COUNSELLING AND PSYCHOTHERAPY IN PRIMARY HEALTH CARE

A Psychodynamic Approach

JAN WIENER

and

MANNIE SHER

MACMILLAN

First published 1998 by
MACMILLAN PRESS LTD
Houndmills, Basingstoke, Hampshire RG21 6XS
and London
Companies and representatives
throughout the world

ISBN 0–333–65205–3
A catalogue record for this book is available
from the British Library.

10   9   8   7   6   5   4   3   2   1
07   06   05   04   03   02   01   00   99   98

Copy-edited and typeset by Povey–Edmondson
Tavistock and Rochdale, England

Printed in Malaysia

CONTENTS

FOREWORD
Andrew Elder

General practitioners are often rather modest about their counselling skills, pretending they know little about counselling and its expertise; but over the years in practice they have usually gained an extensive knowledge of life through witnessing a vast range of different people's reactions to living. This body of experience, with its related set of listening skills can easily get overlooked, particularly in an atmosphere where there is an over-reliance on the more measurable aspects of medicine. But if it is more fully recognised, it can quickly be seen that this aspect of general practice and a psychodynamic approach to counselling (and psychotherapy) are likely to be productive allies. Both are concerned with human development, difficulties in relationships, and with disturbing emotions, pain and distress, but also with the idea that growth and greater resourcefulness can arise out of emotional difficulty. Both are also concerned with the unfolding of longer-term narratives of life, for therapists seen through a window of regular sessions designed to foster an understanding of a person's inner world, and for general practitioners seen through a window of episodic appearances in their consulting rooms for illness and emotional distress, as well as through observing individual patterns of seeking help.

General practice is changing rapidly, but the central difficulties of practising medicine will remain the same: the core continues to be an encounter with suffering and mortality, within the limitations set by a human relationship. This is intensified in general practice, with the inclusiveness of its contract with the patient and the possible timescale of commitment, which can give rise to heavy responsibilities for the GP to carry. Clinical techniques continue to improve, medical organisations develop, and the patterns and emphasis with which professional resources are deployed and change; but all these developments are potentially double-edged. Do we use them to help us perform a difficult task more effectively, or avoid it more easily?

As the responsibilities increase for GPs and primary care teams, each member of the team needs to grow in depth and awareness of the contribution that is made by others. GPs have not been good at this, particularly when relating to professionals outside the medical fold. There is still a need for us to relinquish the 'I can do it all' mentality and learn more about what our colleagues have to offer. This is the only way to prevent teamwork becoming fragmented, and the authors present an excellent model in cross-professional thinking which should help GPs understand much more about the origins, attitudes and aims of counselling. Good medicine and psychodynamic psychotherapy (or counselling) both involve getting to the heart of a problem with someone, and not necessarily taking a long time to do so.

As the authors point out, there has been a steady growth of interest, from the late 1960s onwards, in bringing these two worlds closer together; exploring what the two disciples can bring to each other, and examining the difficulties encountered, because of course there are tensions and differences of approach as well as similarities. To what extent does a therapist become included in shared clinical or organisational thinking within a practice? Welcomed? Or apparently valued but always forgotten about? How is the sharing of information dealt with? Can a sufficiently common language be found to discuss some of the ambivalence and complexities of feeling that tend to cluster around referrals, as well as allowing worthwhile discussion about different roles and an honest formulation of aims?

Until about ten years ago, it was still a relatively small number of practices that employed counsellors or psychotherapists, and they were mainly practices with an already evident interest in a psychological approach to medicine. The number of counsellors working in practices has mushroomed in recent years, and the authors make a number of interesting points about this. The reasons have included the influence of the internal market and the moves to a more primary care based health service, as well as the growth of training in counselling, and (still the most important) the continuing need to bring psychotherapeutic help closer to where most people are likely to be able to benefit from it, when they need it.

Given this longish period of time during which the subject has been developing, and the likely rich potential for therapeutic work in primary care, it may come as something of a surprise that there has not been a comprehensive book of this sort before. But it has been worth waiting, because we do now have a book that has been written from a durable acquaintance with the setting, and from two highly trained analytical psychotherapists who have a real respect for the work, and who were among the first generation of brave therapists who took their skills out into the GP market-place. They have both been involved in teaching and writing about the opportunities presented by GP work for many years. The extent to which they draw on a wide range of psychoanalytic ideas (Feud and Jung in an unusually happy combination), along with concepts drawn from systems theory and organisational consultancy, and the depth with which they are able to relate them to their subject, will not be equalled.

Often in a general practice we are too tightly focused on the immediate and the physical, and less able to shift our focus sufficiently to see other longer-term patterns and feelings unfolding. This tension is ever present in the consulting room, but it is also present in the way the discipline itself is evolving: at one moment seeming to recapture a sense of security by focusing predominantly on an intellectual agenda set within conventional medical lines, and at other times able to be more adventurous and embrace new ways of looking at its work through the eyes of another discipline. *There is much in medicine that cannot be illuminated by medicine alone.* When psychotherapists and GPs work together both should be changed as a result and learn from each other. It is not helpful if doctors use counsellors in order to retreat to 'proper medicine'. Even if some doctors want to do that it does not work, because counsellors can only ever see a fraction of the patients who come to doctors with problems connected to their emotional lives. Such doctors are often mistrustful of theory and what they see as 'soft knowledge', preferring action to talk. The world of counselling will seem foreign to such doctors, and the authors have been wise to use frequent case illustrations which do not allow the text to stray too far into theory, and have the effect of keeping the discussion well-anchored in the recognisable (and always interesting) world of GP surgery problems. This makes it a GP-friendly introduction to the subject for those naturally sceptical GPs.

Just as our understanding of general practice as a discipline continues to evolve as we learn more about the strengths and limitations of our setting, perhaps the same will happen to counsellors and psychotherapists who come to work with us. Doctors start out in general practice with a carefully made bag of skills and knowledge prepared for them in a specialist setting (hospital-based medical schools), and then when they arrive in a surgery they have to begin to adjust, abandoning some things, learning others, until they succeed in finding a way of being a personal doctor in a truly generalist setting. The task for specialists is to be expert within a restricted field, and it can be painful to give up some of the special things that are gained by this, but for some people (not all) other things emerge as a result which make it worthwhile. It will be interesting to see to what extent this process occurs for psychotherapists in primary care. *Will a new and distinct generalist-type primary care therapist begin to appear, with a carefully structured training to match?* As the authors point out, it is misleading to think of this as simple work, requiring little in the way of training. The range of patients encountered, the often-complicated surrounding network of professional relationships, the impact of chronic and serious physical illness, and the need for flexibility and responsiveness to the less regulated and often anxiety driven environment in primary care, all make it a demanding place to work. And if you are going to set sail in a rough sea, you need a well-made craft to carry you. How should it be constructed? For the future I would hope that therapists in practice might have had a well-internalised primary training which has included some experience of working in primary care, before then participating in a programme of further training which focuses on the special aspects of the setting, and subsequently to be able to be part of a continuing and supportive professional network of therapists and doctors too. As is apparent from Appendix B, (Professional Training for Counselling in Primary Care) there is still more or less no further training available for therapists wanting to work (or for those who are already working) in general practice.

It is clear from the authors that this is an exciting new arena for highly effective therapeutic work. And it is largely uncharted territory. Stimulated by reading this book, I found myself wondering whether we have all been rather slow in realising that this is more than simply a change of *place* for counsellors (or psychotherapists) to locate themselves, but something rather more interesting than that, a move that could pave the way for a *distinctive new discipline* with accompanying research interests and clinical expertise? Jan Wiener and Mannie Sher have done an excellent job, but let us hope it turns out to be a foundation-stone raising as many questions for the future as it answers, and paving the way for more detailed studies of the many different aspects of this work to which the authors have shown the way.

For instance, in the light of recent research into the later effects of parent–child interaction arising from attachment theory, should we be beginning to think more about primary care work with children, and with mothers and infants? How can we examine further the effects on psychotherapeutic work of the containing function of a practice? Is there a greater intensity of therapeutic contact possible in the relatively brief but repeated series of sessions in primary care than would be possible in other settings or private practice? In what ways can therapeutic work adapt itself in order to take full advantage of the nature and timescale of the GP setting?

This question is urgent, because of the present unfortunate dominance of the time-limited, six session models, which completely run against the open-door nature of work in general practice, and tend to be driven by anxieties about unlimited need. What can we learn from patients who are unlikely to see a therapist in any other setting? Similarly, what becomes possible because of the opportunity for collaborative work? If there is a sense in which a practice can become a secure base, should we begin to consider the therapeutic (as well as research) implications of the characteristics of a patient's attachment relationship to the practice? And there must be many ways in which we can extend our understanding of psychosomatic medicine. In other words the clinical parameters of work in this setting are still to be defined, and the process is likely to continue generating many interesting questions. Let us hope that the culture of general practice evolves in such a way that undertaking studies of this sort will become more rather than less likely.

We need combined exploration: doctors and therapists together. Both will be the richer as a result. Patients will benefit too. The role is now an established one and the figures show a large number of therapists already working in practices. The time is ripe for more examination of the work, and proper training and research. This book is likely to give the whole subject a major boost, and I welcome it.

ANDREW ELDER
General Practitioner Lisson Grove, London
Consultant in General Practice and Primary Care,
Tavistock Clinic, London

FOREWORD

Bonnie Sibbald

The general practice setting is one of the most challenging environments in which to provide counselling. As the principal providers of primary health care, general practice teams offer first contact, ongoing and comprehensive health care to people irrespective of their age, sex or presenting health problem. A very high proportion of the people presenting in general practice have emotional or psychological difficulties enmeshed within a complex tangle of physical and social problems. The health care team's job is to help people make sense of this undifferentiated distress and *dis*-ease, and formulate a strategy that will foster a return to health and well-being. Counsellors can play an enormously valuable part in this process, but to do so they need to appreciate the special opportunities and limitations of working in primary care teams. Equally, primary health care professionals need to understand and value the counsellor's role if the team as a whole is to work effectively in maximising health outcomes for patients.

The authors, both experienced psychotherapists in primary health care, thoroughly understand and bring alive the special circumstances of work in the general practice setting. They aptly liken general practice to a souk or bazaar in the richness and complexity of presenting problems, the high emotional tension and the absence of firm boundaries. Counsellors new to general practice will find this book helps them make sense of the 'souk'. The culture of general practice, the nature of the doctor–counsellor relationship, and the opportunities and limitations of work in this setting are explained and richly illustrated with case material. For their part, general practitioners and primary health care nurses will find the book offers an invaluable insight into how counsellors work with clients, the philosophies underpinning their approach to health care and the benefits they seek to bring to patients. The insights gained should enable each professional better to understand and appreciate the other's role, so enabling them to work more effectively together for the good of the patient.

The early chapters deal with the evolution of counselling services in general practice settings, the emergence of different models of employment, and how this has shaped the nature of counselling service provision. The history illustrates how the development of counselling services in general practice is intimately bound up with the development of general practice itself. National Health Service policy changes over the past two decades have given general practitioners more power to shape the skill mix of their teams by employing or commissioning other health professionals to work with them in the practice. This, together with wider social and cultural changes fostering a more holistic approach to care, has fuelled a massive expansion in general-practice-based counselling services. General practitioners for the most part now practice in large multidisciplinary teams, of which counsellors are a valued and integral part.

Good multidisciplinary team working is an essential part of good primary health care. The authors see effective team working between counsellor and general practitioners as particularly valuable in that it may compensate for fragmentation of life in society by integrating physical with psychological care. Particular attention is therefore given to the nature of the doctor–counsellor relationship. Through their case material and astute observations, the authors reveal the complexity of these relationships and their implications for patient care. Some doctors are uncomfortable dealing with the emotional and psychological needs of patients and need the counsellor to relieve them of this burden. Others regard emotional care as integral to the work of the general practitioner and may be reluctant to see others take over this aspect of their work. Still others recognise that their skills and time are limited and greatly value the assistance of a skilled mental health professional in managing their workload. Tensions in their personal lives mean that all doctors may sometimes make referrals to the counsellor that reflect their own needs more than those of their patients. The counsellors must maintain a delicate balance between flexibility in responding to these differing needs and firmness in maintaining their own space and identity so that patient care is effectively and appropriately directed. It becomes clear that the doctor–counsellor relationship defies stereotyping as it reflects the emergent understanding of two people engaged in learning about each other's skills and working practices. Jan Wiener and Mannie Sher show how counsellors and general practitioners may go about setting the ground rules for their relationship and then build on this foundation to achieve an effective working alliance.

General practice offers counsellors the opportunity to work with a wide range of psychopathologies and engage clients at an early stage, so preventing progression to more serious or entrenched problems. However the time constraints and imperatives of primary care make it generally inappropriate for counsellors to engage in long-term therapy with all but a few clients. Brief therapy provided over no more than six sessions is typical in general practice settings. Counsellors therefore have to be highly skilled in patient assessment, able rapidly to appraise patients' problems and formulate a suitable course of action. Assessment is arguably the most important role of the counsellor in general practice settings and it is entirely appropriate that Jan Wiener and Mannie Sher devote a whole chapter to this issue.

They identify six main aims of the assessment of process – three of which deal with understanding the patient's problem and formulating a treatment plan, and three of which deal with integrating the patient, the problem and the treatment plan into the wider context of the general practice. It is here that the authors' combined expertise in psychodynamic approaches, which emphasise the two-person relationship, and systemic approaches to organisational behaviour, which are able to locate this dyad within a larger network of relationships, is most telling. They show how the doctor–patient relationship shapes the nature of referral to the counsellor; how the counsellor–patient relationship may be used to understand the true nature of the patient's problem; and how the resources and relationships within and outside the practice shape the treatment options available. The chapter integrates and brings into sharp focus the material presented in earlier chapters on the nature of counsellors' work, working arrangements and relationships within the primary care team.

The final chapter of the book is devoted to a consideration of the value and cost-effectiveness of counselling in general practice settings. Counsellors, their clients and their general practitioner colleagues have few doubts that counselling is of benefit to many people. The problem arises in defining the nature of the benefits, estimating the costs of attaining the benefits, and demonstrating that counselling offers bigger health gains per pound invested than alternative forms of care provision. This is a tall order and research into these issues is still in its infancy. General practitioners and counsellors eager to defend the development of counselling services have pointed to potential cost savings in reduced prescriptions for psychotropic drugs, reduced off-site referral rates to specialist psychiatric services, reduced patient consultation rates and reduced patient relapse rates, to mention but a few. None of these claims have yet been proved, and there is growing evidence against several of them. The defenders of counselling services frequently express anger and frustration with health service researchers for their focus on these measurable and arguably peripheral aspects of service provision. In so doing they forget that they are themselves the authors and advocates of these claims. Counsellors, clients and general practitioners alike need to reflect more carefully on the fundamental benefits of counselling, which surely lie in the personal growth and development of clients. It may well be that these benefits are not 'measurable', but it does not follow that they defy description or valuation. In this respect the authors' call for more and better qualitative research into the counselling process is both timely and appropriate.

BONNIE SIBBALD
Reader in Health Service Research
National Primary Care Research and Development Centre
University of Manchester

ACKNOWLEDGEMENTS

This book would never have moved beyond its conception without the many patients we have seen and tried to help. What we have learned from them, through their willingness to entrust us with their distress and their very individual narratives, forms the cornerstone of the ideas embodied in the text of our book. It is these men, women and children whom we would like to acknowledge first.

Our very special thanks go to Alexis Brook and Jane Dammers, as well as to Mary Barker, Catherine Crowther, Roger Higgs, Robert Gosling, Cecile Muller, Joan Schachter, Jane Temperley and Pierre Turquet, whose wisdom, teaching and support as colleagues and friends over many years have helped the seeds of this project to germinate and grow.

Over the years we have worked with different doctors, psychotherapists, counsellors, researchers and supervisees, all of whom are committed to the development of counselling in primary health care and collaborative work between professionals from different disciplines. We would like to thank the following colleagues: Rachel Adema, Monica Bard, Beatrice Bartlett, Ruth Berkowitz, Anna Brave Smith, Mary Burke, Maureen Chapman, Seok Mee Chua, Geralyn Collins, Clare Corbett, Christopher Cordess, Steven Curson, Gareth Dee, Jan Dereham, Andrew Elder, Brian Fine, Esther Fonseca, Antony Garelick, Haru Ghadiali, Hilary Graham, Raymond Ho, Joan Hutton, Georgia Lepper, Patrick Keane, Patrick Kiernan, Ciaran Kilduff, Tim Ladbrook, Christine Manzi, David Mazure, Barbara McKenzie, Carmel Mond, Helen Muller, Teresa Pawlikowska, Christopher Perry, David Poole, Anne Robinson, Claudette Rosen, Jane Rosoman, Julia Ryde, Sharon Schamroth, Pury Sharifi, Maureen Sheehan, Bonny Sibbald, Bill Smith, Norah Smith, Sam Smith and Jill Walker.

More personally, we offer our special gratitude to Jane Haynes, Judith Hubback, Judy Goodkin and Gordon Lawrence, who gave us the confidence to begin to write, to Stephen Frosh for his intelligent and thorough editing and to Frances Arnold at Macmillan for supporting the idea. To our families and close friends, in particular Steven Kennedy and Leonie Sher, who had to endure our frequent absences and extreme mood swings during the gestation and birth of the book, we offer grateful thanks for their patience.

Last, but by no means least, we are also grateful to Jonathan Barker for his skill in guiding non-technological psychotherapists through the mazes of computer technology and for his forbearance in correcting ever-changing words and sentences, and to Susan Lucks for her administrative support.

The author and publisher are grateful to Oxford University Press for granting permission to quote from Jan Wiener and Jane Dammers' chapter in Jane Keithley and Geoffrey Marsh (eds), *Counselling in Primary Health Care* (1995), to the *Journal of Analytical Psychology* for extracts from Jan Wiener's article 'Looking out and looking in: some reflection on "body talk" in the consulting room' (*JAP*, vol. 39, no. 3), and to Routledge for extracts from Jan Wiener's chapter in Ian Alister and Christopher Hauke (eds) *Contemporary Jungian Analysis: Post-Jungian Perspectives from the Society of Analytical Psychology* (forthcoming).

PREFACE

When beginning to read a book on counselling it is helpful to have an understanding of where the authors are coming from: their background training and interests; belief systems and models of work; theoretical orientation and prejudices as well as their clinical experience. All these have inevitably affected the content and style of the book.

Although we come from different backgrounds – Jan Wiener is a Jungian analyst and research psychologist – and Mannie Sher is a psychoanalytical psychotherapist and organisational consultant – we both have experience of working in similar settings, including the National Health Service, primary care, industry and private practice, and in many ways our skills and experiences are complementary. We hope that, as a team, we have sufficient in common in terms of our attitudes to work in primary care to give a coherence to the central themes in the book, while at the same time sufficient difference to incorporate our own specialisms and particular areas of expertise. A central common experience is that we have both worked as psychotherapists in GP practices for over fifteen years, and it is from our psychological and political commitment to the benefits and exciting opportunities for developing counselling and psychotherapy in primary care, that the energy and motivation to write this book has been generated and sustained over a two year period. Jan Wiener brings particular interests in assessment for counselling and psychotherapy and in the psychodynamics of psychosomatic illness; Mannie Sher brings expertise in the areas of group dynamics and organisational behaviour.

The book is predicated on a psychodynamic approach that places great value on the role of unconscious forces in the shaping of both individual and collective attitudes and behaviour. We believe it likely that the context and general character of primary care fundamentally determine the kind of work that goes on with patients and the dynamics of interpersonal relationships within the primary care team. The challenge for counsellors working in this field lies in trying to combine two approaches: a psychodynamic approach, where the privacy of the two-person relationship between a patient and counsellor is respected, and a systemic understanding of organisational behaviour, as the patient–counsellor dyad is likely to constitute only one part of the network of relationships in the practice as a whole. A systems approach is concerned with how systems influence the delivery of care. Counsellors need to relinquish some of their private practice dictums, which are emphasised in many training courses, if they are to adapt successfully to the work. They need to become more flexible about the models of work they use, their techniques, responsiveness and boundaries of confidentiality.

This book also places considerable emphasis on an object relations approach, where relationships between people in the practice are highly valued. The quality of the relationship between GP and counsellor has a critical effect on the nature of the work with patients, and this relationship is in turn affected by the power of the patient. In an environment where action predominates and where quick decisions are often necessary, our approach advocates a space for thinking and reflecting about what is happening inside the patient, the GP and the counsellor, as well as between them and within the practice as a whole. Many psychodynamic concepts, developed originally by Freud, Jung, Klein, Winnicott, Bion and others, can be very useful in helping counsellors to understand these relationships more profoundly, particularly if they are looked at in the context of personal and institutional defence mechanisms. This understanding, involving time to consider 'what things mean', can lead to better decision making and improved patient care, and constitutes the fulcrum of the approach that is developed in the different chapters of this book.

We hope we have produced a book that is useful for primary health care professionals with an interest in counselling, its appropriateness for patients, its benefits, pitfalls and the different ways in which it may be incorporated into practices. We have written it with the expectation that counsellors, psychotherapists, GPs, psychologists, community psychiatric nurses, health visitors, practice nurses and practice receptionists will all find something to interest them. Whilst an increasing number of papers on counselling in primary care are now being written, the existing literature is generally thin. East (1995) and Keithley and Marsh (1995) have produced valuable texts on the subject, but this is the first single volume to develop the principles and practice of counselling in primary care from a *psychodynamic* point of view.

We do not intend that the book should be read from start to finish. Each chapter is complete in itself and we have cross-referenced topics that appear in different chapters. When learning about any subject there is usually a dialectic between theory and practice, and although our brief was to produce a 'practical' text on counselling in primary health care, as all good practice is underpinned by appropriate theory we have included relevant contemporary psychoanalytic theory that will be useful to the practitioner. A glossary of terms appears in Appendix A at the end of the book. We have included many case examples in all chapters in the hope that this will bring the nature of the work to life. All names and some personal details have been disguised to protect the identity of our patients.

The term 'counsellor' is used throughout, although we are aware that many people working in primary care will be trained as psychotherapists or psychologists and that many counsellors bring the values of psychotherapy and a psychoanalytic approach to their work. Our view is that a psychodynamic approach to individual and institutional work can build a bridge between the fields of counselling and psychotherapy and may be theoretically and clinically useful for both. Similarly, we use the word 'patient', although we know that for many counsellors the designation 'client' is better suited to the nature of their relationship with the people with whom they work.

Debates about the differences between counselling and psychotherapy are commonplace and can become heated. Definitions of counselling range from the generic, which argues in favour of the 'deprofessionalisation of counselling' so that its methods may become widely available, to the narrower definitions in popular use, including 'counselling as advice' and 'counselling in psychological and social care' (Bond, 1995). This latter usage comes closest to the approach developed in this book, where we emphasise the use of the relationship between a trained counsellor and a patient as the central method of facilitating personal growth in the patient.

The BAC (1993, p. 1) also defines counselling in this vein:

> the overall aim of counselling is to provide an opportunity for the client to work towards living in a more satisfying and resourceful way. The term 'counselling' includes work with individuals, pairs or groups of people, often, but not always referred to as 'clients'. The objectives of particular counselling relationships will vary according to the client's

needs. Counselling may be concerned with developmental issues, addressing and resolving specific problems, making decisions, coping with crises, developing personal insight and knowledge, working through feelings of inner conflict or improving relationships with others. The counsellor's role is to facilitate the client's work in ways which respect the client's values, personal resources and capacity for self-determination

The task of differentiating between counselling and psychotherapy is almost impossible, given the many different meanings that are attributed to both terms, as well as the overlap between them. From the inside of the profession looking out, it is probably true to say that we are talking about differences in training, both in approach, where different trainings emphasise and teach different skills, and in intensity, where the length of time, frequency and depth of personal therapy may vary. From our own perspective, it is often the degree of deprivation in the patient's early life and the stage of developmental failure that determine whether counselling or psychotherapy is more appropriate. Although both of us have undergone similar training, and subscribe to a similar approach to working with people in distress, we bring our own perspectives to the job. Struggling to make distinctions in meaning between terms takes us into stormy waters, where the rivalries and status positions among different training organisations can seriously interfere with clarity of thinking. As Bond (1995, p. 7) helpfully points out:

> there is no universally accepted distinction between the terms 'counselling' and 'psychotherapy' . . . there are well-established traditions which use the terms interchangeably. On the other hand, the terms *are* sometimes used in ways which distinguish them from each other.

The BAC (1993, p. 2) acknowledges that:

> a number of differently qualified professionals may fulfil the role of a 'counsellor' in a general practice. These include: counsellors, psychotherapists, nurses, doctors, chartered psychologists and social workers . . . who will bring a variety of different professional skills to the role.

This book applies a psychodynamic approach to work in primary health care and will be of interest to *both* counsellors and psychotherapists who are psychodynamically trained. Attempts to differentiate between counsellors and psychotherapists in terms of their training may therefore be less relevant than attempts to ensure that professionals do not sail into waters beyond their personal training, skills and experience. Regular supervision of clinical work is likely to provide valuable assistance in recognising those problems that can be worked with and those that require greater depth or intensity and a further referral.

At the moment the profession is putting an enormous amount of time and energy into regulating itself and providing national standards and ethical guidelines. The British Association of Counselling is a national body that is working on user guidelines about training standards for counsellors, so that prospective users may know enough about the background qualifications of the counsellors they see to trust that they are sufficiently well-trained. There are plans in motion to start a United Kingdom Register for Counsellors (UKRC). Within the field of psychotherapy there has been much progress towards regulation of the profession. The United Kingdom Council for Psychotherapy (UKCP), whose total membership is approaching 3600, now has a register of 75 organisations offering different types of psychotherapy. These organisations are classified into eight groups according to their approach, and there are stringent procedures for establishing basic standards and codes of ethics. Another organisation, the British Confederation of Psychotherapists (BCP), was formed in 1995 to take account of the more stringent training standards of some psychoanalysts, analytical psychologists and psychoanalytical psychotherapists, and now has twelve member organisations. The two umbrella organisations continue to exist side by side, and a number of psychotherapists belong to both.

JAN WIENER AND MANNIE SHER

HOPES AND REALITIES OF WORK IN A PRIMARY CARE SETTING

The growth of counselling in primary care

Counselling has become a fashionable, multifaceted profession and patients have access to counselling for any one of a number of different problems: HIV counselling, abortion counselling, cancer counselling, counselling for post-traumatic stress syndrome, to name but a few. Along with these specialist services, counselling in primary care has now become an accepted and valued discipline, with counsellors employed in practices in many different parts of the country.

In 1977 the Counselling in Medical Settings (CMS) division of the British Association of Counselling (BAC) was established, reflecting the growth of counselling placements. It started with a membership of around two hundred, but at the time of writing membership has increased to almost seventeen hundred, including a representation from thirty eight different organisations, and it remains the fastest growing division of the BAC. It is difficult to know whether this evolution has occurred as a result of the increasing interest in and relevance of counselling in medical settings, or whether counsellors have always worked in surgeries but without formal recognition. Whichever is true, counselling in primary care has now become integrated into our culture and is here to stay.

GPs today are under pressure – part political, part socio-economic and part personal – to change their working methods, to expand their understanding of illness and to respond with a broader range of options. It is considered necessary to deliver a wider and more comprehensive service to larger numbers of people in a shorter time, and to address newly emerging medical patterns that reflect changing social attitudes. Sexual mores, marriage, the family and divorce, gender and ethnic issues, and economic and employment patterns are all in a state of flux and they have ushered in new attendance at surgeries, placing enormous strain on the traditional providers of primary care. These innovations are having an impact on doctors' personal lives and they are less inclined to manage large workloads alone in long, antisocial working days. They can feel uneasy about the transfer of resources from their direct control into the hands of other specialists, such as the social services or health visitors. The development of a new breed of group practices in the 1960s and 1970s, shifting the emphasis away from the self-managing, independent contractors to joint partnerships, was one way of managing these strains. Doctors in primary care have had to reinvent themselves as members of teams sharing the care of the same patients with their partners, planning on-call rotas, sharing administration, nursing and other facilities and developing specialist skills.

Many practices have offered some kind of direct or indirect counselling for a number of years. Sometimes the GPs themselves do the counselling, at other times it is the practice nurse, the receptionist or, on occasion, the GP's wife who see patients in a pastoral capacity. Keithley and Marsh (1995, p. xiii) alert us to the need for a distinction between 'practising counselling' and 'counselling skills': 'is it best to appoint individuals for whom counselling is their sole activity? Or is counselling something which all those concerned with the health of individuals should see as part of their responsibilities?'

Sibbald *et al.* (1993) carried out the first piece of published research to provide data on the number of counsellors employed in surgeries. They contacted 1880 GPs in England and Wales and discovered that 31 per cent of practices offered some kind of counselling function. Of these, 528 practices reported the on-site presence of a community psychiatric nurse, 266 a practice counsellor, 177 a clinical psychologist, 132 a psychiatrist, 96 a psychiatric social worker and 45 a psychotherapist. They found that on the whole it was the larger group practices that were more likely to employ a counsellor, in particular training practices that ran stress, bereavement or other mental health clinics, and they found that regional employment policies for counsellors were variable and patchy throughout the country.

Counselling in primary health care is unusual in that it has grown in an organic and certainly pluralistic way. Counsellors employed in practices have variable amounts of training and come from training organisations that emphasise a variety of different belief systems. Some practices have accepted offers of placements from professionals in established disciplines, most of whom work at the surgery on a sessional basis; other GPs have chosen to employ counsellors directly from their own budgets, through local Family Health Service Authority (FHSA) reimbursement schemes or through specific counselling initiatives. Because of this the field has been extremely fragmented and it is only now, in the mid 1990s, that real attention is being paid to the specific features of counselling in a primary care setting, the nature of the work, training requirements and contracts of employment.

Sibbald *et al.* followed up their original research with in-depth telephone interviews with a representative sample of 72 GPs and 60 of the counsellors who had participated in the original national survey. The aim of this research study was to 'gain greater insight into the functioning of these (counselling) services in order to determine the most appropriate focus for future research and development' (Sibbald *et al.*, 1996, p. 1). They ascertained that two thirds of counsellors were employed by District Health Authorities (DHAs) and attached to practices and one third were employed by the practice with the financial assistance of FHSAs. Most GPs preferred to employ counsellors themselves as it gave them greater control over who to select and their working arrangements. Counsellors were found to receive referrals principally from GPs and occasionally from other primary health care staff. Self-referral by patients was rare. The problems for which patients were most commonly referred included stress/anxiety, relationship problems, depression and bereavement. The principal therapeutic styles were Rogerian counselling, behaviour therapy and psychodynamic psychotherapy. One quarter of the counsellors described their style as 'eclectic'. Individual, rather than group or family therapy was the norm. Overall, 28 per cent of counsellors were found to hold no formal qualification in counselling or any of the psychotherapies. Counsellors and GPs were generally satisfied with the service and the main problem seemed to be that demand always exceeded capacity.

Why this growth? Implications of social change

Good GPs have always known that they need to attend to the psychological as well as the physical problems of their patients. However the old Cartesian splits, where care of the body is allocated to one discipline and concern for the mind to another, run deep and many GPs have neither the training, the time nor the interest to make themselves fully available to attend to their patients' psychological difficulties. To concentrate on 'the body' could be said to be sufficient, the more familiar and straightforward option.

The evolution of the primary care service reflected the volume of work and nature of the medical problems experienced, and it was recognised that primary care structures would have to adapt. Without losing sight of the fundamental principle that the interests of the individual patient were paramount, doctors were influenced by new organisational theories that portrayed families as systems and asserted the interdependence of the diverse parts of the primary care system. This meant that doctors who had previously worked with patients holistically now found their work fragmented by operational systems that were much larger and more difficult to control. The dual burden of viewing marriages and families as systems, while at the same time being just one part of a larger primary health care mechanism, proved stressful for doctors. They felt that they were becoming small cogs in a vast machine and that their traditional models of medical practice were becoming outmoded.

By the early 1970s a few group practices – mainly in inner London boroughs – took advantage of the training offered by the Tavistock Clinic (Balint, 1964; Bourne, 1976; Brook, 1967, 1974; Brook and Temperley, 1976; Graham and Sher, 1976; Sher, 1977; Temperley, 1978) to deepen GPs' understanding of their patients' psychological difficulties and their role in boosting their patients' psychological well-being. Psychologists, psychiatrists and social workers in the Adult Department of the Tavistock Clinic were seconded to GP practices in north-west London for one or two sessions per week, where they assessed patients believed to be in need of psychological help, and consulted with the surgery staff on the psychological aspects of their patients' symptoms. These placements were the forerunners of a movement to offer psychotherapeutic services to larger sections of the population and in greater numbers than could be seen in specialist psychotherapy clinics. Over the next twenty years an increasing number of GP practices in London and other cities, now called primary health care teams, began to include psychotherapists and counsellors. This 'movement' was both welcomed and criticised. Sometimes the efficacy of having psychotherapy services on health centre premises was questioned and doubt cast on the usefulness of the 'talking treatment' in alleviating neurotic and personality disorders (Corney and Briscoe, 1977; Forman and Fairbairn, 1968; Ratoff and Pearson, 1970; Goldberg and Neill, 1972).

In the last few years there has been a considerable increase in the number of patients who present with mental health problems. Shifts in mental health resources from the hospitals out into the community have meant that GPs are increasingly faced with large numbers of patients with emotional, social and psychiatric problems, such as stress-related illness, unemployment, divorce or single parenting. The pressures are huge, and it is therefore not surprising that GPs are sharing the responsibility, which might include employing a counsellor in the practice. The trends away from single-handed practices towards the formation of larger group practices that offer a range of different specialist services have provided opportunities for the development of teamwork approaches to primary care. Professionals from different backgrounds – including health visitors, practice nurses, counsellors and, sometimes, practitioners of complementary medicine – can work together creatively.

A mixed response to counselling

The expectations of counselling services parallels general medical trends. Both can be seen as a reaction to the loss of a sense of continuity with the past and the future, as well as a reflection of the decline in alternative forms of institutional support such as religion and the family. This loss of institutional support has been responsible for generating insatiable and undiscriminating social and emotional needs. As a result, patients' expectations of what counselling can do for them are often artificially high and based on false hopes. Counselling can be perceived as an exclusive encounter for paying patients in private practice or in specialist NHS psychotherapy clinics. Counsellors can be regarded as omniscient, or imbued with magical powers – an image with which counsellors sometimes wishfully identify. The demand is for the *maternal* giving of counselling rather than for the *paternal* authority of medicine, since notions of authority, leadership and power are often seen to form no part of the counsellor's role. The public seek counselling as an expression of its new, generalised 'dissatisfaction-with-self' mood, and it is particularly popular among people wishing to enrich their lives and become more effective. But although there are many who embrace counselling of their own volition, the main demand in primary care is for help and support for the ill, the disturbed and those unable to cope. In these cases it is often the GP who takes the initiative.

The huge changes in the structures of primary care already mentioned mean that GPs have to spend more time on political and administrative activities, often at some cost to their clinical duties and leaving even less time to attend to mental health problems. Hinshelwood (1996) has written articulately about the shifts in the medical and mental health professions from 'patient-anxiety' towards 'market-anxiety'. GPs are having to adjust to fund-holding status and increases in their purchasing power and authority, which regrettably may lead to treatment options based on economics rather than good medical or psychological sense. In this atmosphere it is difficult to know whether counsellors are increasingly employed because they are needed and seen as good value for money, or whether GPs have come to appreciate more fully the benefits for their patients of time to talk and a space for reflection.

Both authors have noticed during their employment in primary care that many more patients are now making direct requests for counselling. It has certainly become more acceptable to seek professional help for mental disturbance or unhappiness, which might previously have been dealt with by a visit to a priest, expressed as a physical problem or simply ignored (Miller *et al.*, 1983). By the 1950s pain was no longer accepted as an inescapable part of the human condition. It was defined as a deviation from the norm and there was an expectation that a GP with 'a pill for every ill' ought to be able to cure it. However during the 1960s there was much greater concern with personal development, growth of the self and the abandonment of inhibitions. Primary care responded to these shifts in societal values and needs, and also helped to legitimise them by introducing new people with specialist skills to assist in the realisation of these goals. Multidisciplinary teamwork was established in primary care and was no longer the preserve of hospitals and clinics, where it had been established for many years.

It is surely not just the presence of a counsellor in the practice that makes counselling more accessible, but rather that patients now expect their GPs to provide some kind of psychological help when they are in distress. Elder's (1996, p. 62) description of the work of a GP is apt:

> in the surgery, we live closer to the relatively undifferentiated ways in which human suffering and need is expressed. GP consultations are often straight in from the High Street. Any starting point is acceptable, and there are few constraints about the territory that might be travelled

. . . Connections between otherwise-unseen aspects of the patient's life and relationships, past and present, or between body and mind, may become more evident, often to the surprise and enlivenment of both the patient and the doctor.

For doctors, the presence of counsellors in the team can spell a reduction in their patient counselling roles. While lack of time is often the chief justification for GPs to limit their work to the treatment of physical symptoms, the loss of the informal counselling role has been responsible for lowering their job satisfaction and morale. Furthermore medical training, which pays less attention to the GP–patient relationship, may reinforce the GPs' roles as biological technicians, resource manipulators and traffic controllers. Understandably, therefore, arrival of counsellors on the primary care scene was met with mixed feelings. On the one hand GPs were pleased that their patients would receive emotional support in times of stress and relieved that counselling for the more neurotic, time-wasting patients could be passed on to someone else, but on the other hand, they felt resentful that the emotional dimension of care was being diverted away from them towards specially trained personnel. They were being turned into technical operators of somatics, and were in danger of losing their ability to relate to patients holistically. Not surprisingly, then, counsellors' ability to produce symptom relief, help depression, avert hysterical conversion and restore sexual functioning by means of empathic attention to patients' distress produced a mixed reaction in doctors: pleasure and reassurance that a new dimension of health care was being made available to their patients, and consternation, a feeling of rivalry and not a little envy that counsellors were producing results that doctors themselves wished they could emulate (see Chaper 2 below on the doctor–counsellor relationship).

Attractions of the work

What, the reader may ask, are the attractions of this work? The commitment of both authors to writing a book on the subject suggests that the attractions are powerful, and from our own experience they may be described under five main headings.

Working at the coalface

The rewards of participating in a process at its inception are compelling. It is to their GP that patients usually take their problems in the first instance. Thus counsellors can work with problems when they are fresh, presenting real opportunities to prevent reactive disorders from becoming chronic. While the coalface inevitably brings a dirty, darker side with many pressures to do the most in the least possible time, primary care is 'the real world' of mental health problems, where counsellors are forced to learn how to use all the psychodynamic and management skills they possess appropriately and flexibly.

Seeing a wide variety of patients

A more diverse range of patients is likely to be seen by the counsellor working in primary care than in most other settings, and certainly more diverse than in private practice. For counsellors who wish to broaden their clinical experience and improve their assessment skills, this environment is a rich resource. Working in an institution with colleagues on site means that the counsellor feels sufficiently secure to work with potentially more disturbed patients, as well as encountering patient populations who are less likely to present to private practices, such as those from ethnic groups, elderly patients and patients with entrenched psychosomatic difficulties. The setting provides many opportunities to work with couples and families with young children and adolescents, as well as the more usual one-to-one counselling.

Working as part of a team

For the counsellor working alone in the rather introverted atmosphere of private practice, working in a practice team alongside different health professionals provides a refreshing breath of fresh air. Clinical and philosophical discussions with colleagues, particularly those trained in a different discipline, always inform our thinking and our practice. Compared with the tightly boundaried dyadic model of private practice, true teamwork involves exciting opportunities for shared care of patients who are best helped when the doctor and the counsellor work closely and collaboratively to manage and treat their problems.

Flexibility of workstyle

A primary care environment demands that counsellors experiment with different styles of work. The central attitude to the work, in this case a psychodynamic way of thinking about patients and institutions, is likely to remain constant, but the fact that the demand for counselling almost always exceeds the supply means that counsellors must make creative use of their time, involving the need really to think about what is best for patients. Training-led dogmas such as 'six sessions for all patients' or 'once a week counselling or nothing' may provide a containing structure for counsellors or those who fund the placements, but they may not necessarily be in the patients' best interests. Many patients are well served by less regular sessions or even shorter sessions.

Missionary work

Counsellors who work in primary care are in an ideal place to build bridges with other disciplines, to take their own specialism 'out into the community' and make it available, albeit in a modified form, to other professionals. Counsellors can offer GPs, practice nurses and health visitors new and different perspectives about patients, families or situations of concern to the practice as a whole. The rewards of such liaisons, where different perspectives about patients' communications may be absorbed, leading to the integration of new ideas and changes in rituals of practice, are truly gratifying and keep motivation for the work buoyant.

CASE EXAMPLE: DR JONES

A GP complains to the counsellor about the number of her patients who repeatedly return to her surgery telling her that they feel no better, whatever treatment she recommends. The counsellor suggests that the next time such a patient presents, the GP should try saying something like: 'you are making me feel as if everything I do is unable to help you adequately'. Some days later the GP reports back to the counsellor that upon saying this to a male patient, the patient had said: 'but you are the doctor, you should be able to help'. The GP then found herself able to think about the patient's dependency problems and free herself from her own identification with the 'inadequate doctor' projection, and hence find a more constructive language with which to talk to the patient about identifying ways in which they could work together to alleviate his distress.

CASE EXAMPLE: THE RECEPTIONISTS

During a monthly meeting with their counsellor, the GPs ask the counsellor's advice about how to manage their receptionists. They have recently received a number of complaints that members of the reception staff are being rude to patients. The counsellor asks why the doctors seem anxious about talking to the receptionists about this problem. This question provokes the realisation among the anxious GPs that they are dependent on their receptionists to act as their henchmen to keep difficult patients and situations at bay. They are frightened to tackle them for fear that there might be a row and the receptionists will hand in their notice. The counsellor points out that this is only one possibility and that the receptionists might actually welcome a discussion about how to manage difficult patients. However when the GPs ask the counsellor (who is employed directly by the practice) to run a workshop to teach the receptionists communication skills, she declines, on the basis that she too has occasionally experienced rudeness by the receptionists, and because she is employed by the practice it will be more sensible to buy in outside help. The counsellor suggests a suitable person and an afternoon training session is arranged.

Both the above examples illustrate the potential for productive collaborative work between counsellors and GPs if a trusting relationship exists between them. They also illustrate the usefulness of a psychodynamic understanding of the less conscious aspects of relationships between doctor and patient and between members of the practice team. Working in a practice with different health professionals is both exciting and challenging, always providing interesting new patients, different experiences and problems, new reflections about how to deal with them and the potential for counsellors to develop and mature personally and professionally. A psychodynamic approach that includes an understanding of institutional dynamics is likely to facilitate this process.

The character of the setting

A GP practice is usually a chaotic place in which to work. GPs lead busy lives, need to make quick decisions and are notoriously inefficient at creating and maintaining space in which to reflect about the work they do. Blake Morrison's (1993, p. 9) description of his father, who was a GP, illustrates this: 'my father does not like waiting in queues. He is used to patients waiting in queues to see him, but he is not used to waiting in queues himself'. It could be said that this constitutes an institutional defence against anxiety, as to internalise all the worries of the considerable number of patients seen during each surgery would surely be overwhelming.

As a working environment, the surgery has particular character-istics. The metaphor of a *home* – a local place to which people go at many different times during their lives with a range of life-stage-relevant problems – is useful here. Many patients have a close relationship with their GPs, often extending over many years. Ten times as many people with mental health problems are seen in primary care as in the specialist psychotherapy or psychology services, and counsellors working on site in a practice can directly and indirectly influence members of the practice team when it comes to the emotional aspects of patients' presenting problems. Another metaphor used to describe the atmosphere of primary care is that of a *souk* (Wiener, 1996, p. 68):

> an Arab souk or bazaar, where everything is potentially available, is like a practice, where GPs have to maintain a gate-keeping function with often limited resources. GPs have to cope with whoever walks through the door and must decide what is treatable and what must be borne or managed.

This may be compared with the more specialised outpatient psy-chotherapy clinic where the atmosphere is more like a *citadel*:

> an army of therapists working inside a citadel, with a strong outer wall surrounded by sentries . . . . The erection of a citadel may be the only means by which therapeutic integrity can be maintained, however, such an active gate-keeping function involving stringent referral procedures, long waiting lists and often minimal communication with GPs, will not necessarily help to foster good relationships between these services and primary care (ibid., p. 68).

For a counsellor who works on site in a practice and comes from a training background where firm boundaries and structures are advocated, adjusting to work in this particular setting can be slow and trying. Counsellors are working in a much more porous atmo-sphere than the rarefied culture of private practice, and may need to be vigilant to forces from several different directions that can impinge on their work. These can include pressure to take on a huge number of referrals; negotiations with members of the practice staff who have different expectations of the role of the counsellor; practice administrators who are reluctant to take any responsibility for the administrative needs of the counsellor; or difficulties in creating and maintaining a private space in which to work. In general these constitute strong pressures for counsellors to become like GPs and they may have to struggle to maintain a delicate balance between flexibility in terms of work style (the souk) and firmness in order to maintain a space to retain their own identity (the citadel), so that the assessment and treatment process may develop satisfactorily.

A primary care setting affords the opportunity for a number of different things, previously separate, to come together. Psyche and soma may become more integrated; people from two different professional backgrounds can learn to work together and to learn each other's languages. For a counsellor there is an opportunity to integrate a wider range of different patient psychopathologies with the more traditional private practice approach that emphasises the unique character of each individual patient. In private practice, counsellors may have paid less attention to psychopathology and concentrated more on helping their patients to grow and understand themselves better. In primary care, where assessment is a fundamental part of the work, both counsellor and GP working together may be forced to pay more attention to psychopathology and resources as important elements in decisions about future treatment.

GPs and counsellors working together

The context of primary care, whilst potentially fruitful, is likely to highlight some of the differences between GPs, with their medical training, and counsellors, with their psychological training. In general there is a cultural gap that can make liaison and communication between the two professionals difficult. This is particularly relevant in a decade when *collaborative care* is the common theme in so many NHS initiatives. East's description of the atmosphere of the medical world may ring bells for the new counsellor:

> the medical world can be likened to a tribal village society . . . a culture with a rich recorded history in addition to its folklore, which has a

complex system of values and beliefs and an established educational system rooted in science, but also responsive to sponsorship and patronage by the elders and others who offer funds for research . . . . Newcomers – and a counsellor in a medical setting is a newcomer – are often regarded with suspicion and hostility. Acceptance and incorporation into village life can take more than one generation (East, 1995, p. 26).

How can counsellors develop their specialist services in ways that are more flexible and usable for GPs without compromising their own value systems? Tensions between different groups of professionals operating in their own work environments, who have different languages, training, hierarchical and vocational structures, are probably inevitable and consciousness about this requires constant vigilance. Tension mitigates against teamwork, which then becomes 'processional' rather than 'integrated' (ibid., p. 15). Patients become the 'recipients of' rather than the 'partners in' care, and the stepping stones for patients can remain far apart. It is only if GPs and counsellors can truly learn to work together that teamwork and better patient care become possible. East believes this will only happen if there can be dialogue between professionals and patients: 'the most appropriate counselling takes place when everyone is clear what is on offer, and what is on offer has been chosen by providers and by consumers. But this is often influenced by counselling meaning different things to different people' (ibid., pp. 130/131). She expresses the task for counsellors most elegantly: 'counsellors must walk the tightrope of being collaborative and communicative, while rigorously maintaining the overriding ethic of confidentiality for their clients' (ibid., p. 131). (See also Chapter 8 below on key professional issues.)

Traditionally, doctors have been in a superior position and their right to control and guard their own territory is taken for granted. In general, irrespective of the background discipline and training of counsellors and the number of hours they work in the practice, the doctor is the key player in a clinical situation. The counsellor is an agent of the GP and treats patients on behalf of the medical system. These are the central operational boundaries between the two disciplines.

Psyche and soma

Whilst GPs recognise that as many as 70 per cent of the problems with which patients present have an emotional component, in reality the structure of primary care makes it difficult to deal adequately with emotional distress. The ten-minute consultation makes it almost impossible for GPs fully to attend to patients who present with complex emotional problems. It is only the more interested GPs who are willing to offer the time to treat psychological problems themselves, rather than referring patients on to specialists. Campkin is one such GP:

> it seems that our society is even more reliant on the family physician to perform functions ranging from those of the priest to those of the grandparent. Consultations requiring counselling as well as clinical skills continue to increase . . . . Counselling is a way of 'being with' patients; not so much a process, more a state of mind. For the doctor with this attitude and aptitude, it is not an optional extra, but as integral to the consultation as history-taking, diagnosis and treatment and may play a part in all these activities (Campkin, 1995, p. 259).

A counselling placement in the practice, if it is working well, provides exciting opportunities to work with patients with psychosomatic illnesses. Traditionally, of the large percentage of patients presenting with psychosomatic complaints, a number begin what might be seen to be an endless series of specialist referrals for different symptoms. Some are both against and unsuited to any kind of 'talking help', preferring a hands-on approach such as physiotherapy, massage or acupuncture. They only find reassurance in medication given by the GP (see Chapter 7 on psychosomatic illness). Other patients are more likely to accept a referral to the practice counsellor, knowing that the counsellor will work closely with the GP to manage their problems, and it is here that much good collaborative work can be done. Similarly, patients and their families who are trying to come to terms with a diagnosis of serious organic disease, possibly terminal, may find support from a counsellor working closely with their GP.

The nature of the relationship between psyche and soma is mysterious and to some extent unfathomable, and it remains unclear why some people respond to stress or trauma by developing a physical symptom while others become depressed or anxious. Elder (1996, p. 60), puts it beautifully: 'the mind – in general practice – just like the mind in life – is inseparable from the body and the two are frequently muddled up, the mind speaking for the body at one moment and the body speaking for the mind at others'.

Counsellors offer GPs opportunities to improve their diagnostic skills and treatment management plans for patients suffering from psychosomatic illness. They can help GPs to distinguish those who could benefit from some form of psychological treatment from those who would be best served by regular, supportive meetings with the GP in the practice. Counsellors are often more comfortable with the 'containment only approach', whereas GPs may perceive those patients for whom past treatment decisions have been insufficient, as a medical failure. In contrast GPs can help counsellors understand more about the medical aetiology of symptoms, a subject much neglected in many counselling training courses.

A counsellor on site in a surgery means that the deep historical splits between mind and body are, in the best of all possible worlds, less likely to occur, and this will have indirect benefits for individual GPs and the surgery as a whole. Those GPs who are more comfortable working with organic illness will gradually acquire a clearer definition of the counsellor's role, part of which may be to say: 'this is not my territory'. Good referrals *can* be made when there are clear lines of demarcation between the work specifications of different professionals. Other GPs will become more psychologically minded, particularly if they allow themselves to develop a relationship with the counsellor.

Core discipline and patterns of employment

Counsellors' professional identity is likely to be affected by their core discipline and the authority that employs them. Different employment arrangements bring different aims and expectations to the surgery.

Counsellors with no core discipline are likely to be employed by the Family Health Service Authority (FHSA) or directly by GPs. Some FHSAs decide the terms and conditions of employment for counsellors: their job descriptions, accountability, tasks and rates of pay. GPs rely on the FHSA's recommendations and may restrict their involvement to selection of a counsellor. The GPs may have a reasonably clear idea of the role of the counsellor and what sort of cases he or she is likely to work with.

In other cases the practice counsellor will be employed by the local trust or will be a psychologist seconded by the psychology department of the local psychiatric or general hospital. This arrangement may also represent an attempt by psychology departments to be more outward-looking and community-orientated. Here the role of psychologist/counsellor is often more focused, leading to contact with patients suffering from conditions that are traditionally associated with treatment by psychologists: obsessive compulsive disorders, eating disorders, phobias or specific sexual problems. These are often behavioural conditions that usually respond well to more structured behavioural treatment.

With the burgeoning of interest in counselling in primary care, several organisations (LIZ money, Tomlinson Funds, Counselling in Primary Care Trust and so on) have donated money that health authorities can use to fund the employment of counsellors. These placements have strings attached. Counsellors so funded are accountable to the funding authority and open to scrutiny by its researchers. Most have a specific focus and the length of employment is finite. The emphasis is on targeted projects in inner-city areas, low-income groups and multicultural communities.

A much smaller group of specialist counsellors are psychiatrists who visit surgeries and give advice about patients with psychiatric illness. Psychiatrists' training in psychotherapy often includes a period of applied work in primary care. They are seconded by their employing trusts and may see patients in the primary care setting in order to make a diagnosis and offer suggestions to the GP for further care. It is rare for these psychiatrist/counsellors to treat patients in the surgery, and they will probably suggest referral to the local hospitals, where more resources and specialist services are available.

Sessions in the surgery

Counselling attachments range from three hours a week to a full five days. On average attachments are for between one and three days. The amount of time available influences what can be achieved. A counsellor employed for up to seven hours per week is not able to do more than three assessments and three follow-up interviews or brief counselling interventions, as one hour is usually reserved for administration, writing notes and meetings. A counsellor employed for two and a half or more days has the opportunity to create a broader service that includes assessment, follow-up and brief treatments. Diversification of the work is possible by including marital, family and group work as part of the overall service. The half-time counsellor may also supervise a trainee counsellor, which if successful is likely to add a further four to six hours to the counselling time available (see Chapter 5 on counselling options).

Summary

At the present time, in spite of the enormous variability of counsellor attachments and the patchwork quality of training and practice and methods, counselling in primary health care has matured sufficiently to become a distinct form of service for patients. It looks as if it is here to stay. Almost everyone involved – patients, doctors and the counsellors themselves – believe that the service is beneficial, cost-effective and an efficient way of addressing mental health problems in the community. The provision is being widely researched and some critical questions are being asked.

It seems likely that the growth of counselling has evolved as both an outside-in movement and an inside-out movement. Changes in government policy have led to changes in the structure of primary health care that make it possible for more counsellors to be employed, and in tandem with this trend we now live in a culture where it is no longer shameful to ask for help with emotional problems, and where the existence of an inner-world and the possibility that emotional stress can be linked to physical illness are well proven. Denis Pereira Gray summarises the benefits of counselling:

> counsellors offer four immediate and obvious advantages. First, they provide another pair of hands to cope with the load; secondly, they are seen as a cheaper and less expensive resource than providing a highly trained doctor to handle what many believe are essentially incurable conditions; thirdly, counselling is systematically geared to talking rather than treating and appeals to those who are concerned about the costs and effects of taking drugs. Fourthly, the issue of helping patients to come to terms with their situation is inherently attractive and less likely to breed dependency on a primary care service (Pereira Gray, 1996, p. v).

Whether the roots of the growth in counselling in a primary care setting are personal, social, cultural or political, the relationship between counsellor, GP and patient is potentially mutually fruitful. The presence of a counsellor in the practice offers the opportunity to expand the psychological resources of the practice as a whole and represents an attempt to keep psyche and soma connected at all levels, and thus to mend the ruptures that have existed for so many years. GPs can provide counsellors with usable medical knowledge to complement their psychological skills, as well as valuable information about a wide range of different patients with whom counsellors would otherwise be unlikely to come into contact.

We expect more today from all the staff in primary care than ever before, and there is every reason for counsellors to be valued as team members. They have specialised training in personality development, child care, family dynamics, group work, community resources, individual, group and organisational psychopathology and therapeutic methods. They bring to bear a unique combination of technical and personal skills in the service of patient care.

2

THE DOCTOR–COUNSELLOR RELATIONSHIP

Setting the scene

Counsellors in primary care are thought to be a good thing (Waydenfeld and Waydenfeld, 1980; Diekstra and Jensen, 1988; House, 1993; Jewell, 1993; Dammers and Wiener, 1995). In Chapter 1 we described the opportunities their presence provides for people to talk about their personal and family problems with someone trained, impartial and sympathetic. More patients now accept that stress relief can be obtained by talking to someone about themselves, their lives and personal problems. In this chapter we focus on the nature of the relationship between GP and counsellor.

How does this 'marriage' between GPs and counsellors come about? What shift in attitudes and resources has to happen before counsellors become more commonplace in primary care? Traditionally patients have looked to their GPs for help with emotional, relationship and family tensions, namely the problems of living, and from them they have received advice, reassurance, support, an ear to listen and a shoulder to cry on. Many GPs enjoy this aspect of their work, believing it to be the essence of good doctoring; others feel ill-equipped to deal with it, and not a few feel unsympathetic, even antipathetic, towards their patients' emotional lives.

Models of teamwork in primary care

The new pairing of doctor and counsellor brings together and positively reinforces the inevitable but overoptimistic 'rescue fantasy' that is inherent in medicine and counselling. We all hope that the difficulties of life, the frailties of our bodies and our flagging spirits will somehow be dealt with by someone else. It is not possible to understand the nature of the new team of doctor and counsellor in primary care without an awareness of Klein's (1935) idea of the depressive position: the realisation that the object of our projected fantasies, and often our hope for salvation, is human like ourselves, and may fail to provide the magic solutions that we seek. In illness, as in other aspects of our lives, we fear the influence of anonymous forces. Doctors are therefore invested with our omnipotence and omniscience. The whole medical system has salvation projected into it, and by opening the system to counsellors they too become imbued with salvationist fantasies. Faith in the counsellors (Halmos, 1965) could be in danger of replacing faith in medicine and religion for individuals who are isolated from their families and communities and who experience intense feelings of loneliness, confusion and an absence of meaning in their lives. This is seen in the large number of patients who present themselves to the practice in a fragmented state.

The model of teamwork we advocate in this book for application in primary care settings is an attempt to compensate for the fragmentation of life in society, in that it places side by side two professionals who, by working together, may be better able to help integrate the physical and psychological aspects of their patients' needs. If patients cannot hold together the disparate parts of their world, then the professionals and the organisations behind them may have to 'hold' those different parts temporarily on their behalf.

CASE EXAMPLE: MARY

Mary is referred by her GP to the counsellor because she is depressed, after several recent illnesses, including an infected shoulder, chest pains and gallstones. Mary, a 39 year old mother of three children and a nurse by profession, has agreed with her GP that she is probably depressed because of these illnesses. The counsellor wonders why the patient is there if both GP and patient agree that she is probably in a depressive post-illness phase. Why has the GP not simply provided her with medication, as is the case with other depressed patients? The counsellor thinks there must be other reasons why an exploration of the patient's situation is desirable.

When the patient is asked about her personal and domestic situation she becomes edgy, catches her breath and says that she had hoped she would not be asked that question. The counsellor says nothing and waits. Moments later the patient's eyes fill with tears and she weeps uncontrollably, unable to breathe properly or speak. She tries to regain her composure, and in between sobs she says that she has lost everything – her home, her clothes, her dignity and pride – because her husband has gambled away all their money and assets. He was in a business that had done well in the good years of the 1980s, but during the recession his addiction to gambling had worsened. She had felt she could not stop him because she did not 'want to deprive her children of a father'. She describes her own child-hood experience of poverty in a large family where her father was unemployed and an alcoholic.

Gentle attempts by the counsellor to help the patient see a possible connection between her feelings about these past events and the current situation are met with incredulity and a return to the idea that her illnesses are causing her depression. The counsellor then makes a more emphatic connection be-tween the patient's stressful life and her illnesses, and draws attention to the intolerable physical and emotional load she is carrying. Mary continues to weep but says she can now under-stand what the counsellor is saying. The counsellor offers another appointment and says he will confer with Mary's GP to review her medication and arrange for some treatment with an osteopath. On leaving the patient says she feels a lot better for talking about these things, which she has kept buried 'as a kind of penance', and is grateful for the help her doctor and counsellor are providing.

In this case example the GP and the counsellor were required to work as a team to hold the split between bodily symptoms and emotions, until such time as the patient, with firm help from the counsellor, was able to move from fragmentation to linking.

Styles of team membership

Models of teamwork in primary care generally depend on how roles, boundaries and the relationships between them are arranged:

- One model is predicated upon the idea that physical problems are dealt with by the GP and psychological and emotional problems by the counsellor. This model, which makes a clear division between psyche and soma, thus replicating the old

Cartesian splits (see Chapters 1 and 7), is likely to mean that the GP and counsellor will rarely confer with each other.

- A second model upholds the firm belief that links between the physical and the psychological are crucial and closely interrelated, meaning that patients will benefit from the GP and counsellor working closely together at every stage of treatment.

CASE EXAMPLE: TRACY

Tracey, a young teenage girl, has been referred because of an unplanned pregnancy, which requires the GP and counsellor to be in constant touch with each other so that proper arrangements can be planned for a number of possible options including (1) the birth of her child, (2) termination of the pregnancy, (3) counselling as a preparation for motherhood, (4) possible adoption or (5) family work with the girl and her parents.

It would be impossible sensitively to help this young girl to make a decision about her future if GP and counsellor were constrained by their identification with a purely physical or a purely psychological approach, respectively.

Against teamwork

Those who oppose the development of doctor–counsellor teams (Martin and Mitchell, 1983; Andrews, 1993; Fahy and Wessley, 1993) argue that:

- Counselling is marginal to the needs of primary care patients.
- There is an uneasy relationship between counselling and medicine. Medicine is regarded as the 'establishment' and counselling as 'new' and 'untested'.
- Unlike medicine, counselling is not based on rational scientific principles and it therefore resembles religion, art or magic.
- Counsellors operate in fairly closed-system consulting rooms because of their feeling of antipathy towards institutions.

Critics of primary care counselling also argue that there may be a serious mismatch between demand and supply, namely that the psychodynamic, one-to-one treatment that is offered by the majority of counsellors is only appropriate for a minority of patients and irrelevant to the rest. Moreover it has been suggested that even if a range of counselling approaches and skills are offered, counsellors lack the capacity to match the appropriate technique with the specific needs of the patient.

Early critics of counselling attachments (Corney, 1990) raised questions about the competence of counsellors and this is closely related to issues of evaluation and accountability, the subjects of perennial debate. Society has a right to expect counselling to be organised, but since at present the profession tends to be disorganised, it is not always easy to ascertain where accountability lies. These doubts also inhibit attention to wider questions about the nature of counselling and its role in primary care, and can contribute to uncertainty about professional identity (see Chapter 9 'Does Counselling Work?').

The wish for perfect care

The wish for perfect care is reciprocal. Both doctors and patients wish to achieve it. However many doctors feel unsure about their roles and recognise that in many areas of human frailty traditional medicine has failed or is insufficient. While the past few decades have seen huge advances in disease prevention, surgery and drug safety, this has been paralleled by a diminution of the close doctor–patient relationship. Yet patients continue to demand and expect 'perfect care', while government pronouncements attempt to set their expectations at more realistic levels. This highlights the contradiction between the unconscious fantasy of perfect mothering, the *perfectly dependable object* that the public seeks, against the reality of limited resources in a priority system. In turn the primary care system would like to see itself as able to cater to all its patients' needs, and cannot resist an unconscious wish to be that 'perfect parent' who nurtures the needy individuals in its care. In spite of all the expectations invested in the relationship, the outcome on both sides is disappointment. This in turn leads to dissatisfaction among patients and a feeling of uselessness among primary care staff. This picture will persist for as long as these underlying fantasies are allowed to gain currency. While doctors and patients continue to believe that the State, as expressed through the NHS, will cure all ills, the outcome cannot but be disappointing. To add to this, members of the primary care team are likely to carry, as part of the resulting countertransference, inexpressible feelings of their own that include aggressive or punitive impulses towards patients for making them feel inadequate and useless.

CASE EXAMPLE: BILL

Sixty five year old Bill habitually draws attention to himself through the use of engaging humour, all cuttingly directed against himself. His self-deprecating remarks are irresistibly funny, but, behind the humour lie alarming thoughts of murder and suicide. His dreams are filled with images of death, but they are related melodiously and amusingly to the GP and counsellor, often forcing them to lose control of their composure and laugh out loud. The patient talks comically about his despair and his desire to kill a man who supplanted him in the affections of the children next door, since when his only wish has been to die. Both GP and counsellor fail to take his death-wish seriously. Only his humour was heard. Dazzled by it, the surgery team think he is not serious, and consequently the required attention is not offered to him. Clearly the team has become so thoroughly seduced by the patient's main defence mechanism, his sense of humour, that they are completely ignoring his feeling of hopelessness. In their distraction, they let him wander off without confronting his great self-destructive potential.

CASE EXAMPLE: RICHARD

The second case illustrates how the responses of professional staff may reflect their patient's inner state. Richard who is 27, frightened and agitated, recites a long list of short unsatisfactory jobs, from which he either walked out or was fired. He has a girlfriend and a child and they live on income support. Work is no longer an option for him, because he will be financially worse off if he loses his benefits. He hints at certain events in his history to account for his low emotional state, but refuses to elaborate on them. He says he fantasises all day about how things might have been for him 'had certain other things not happened'. The patient diverts all attempts to confront his complaints about how others have complicated his life. He shows no inclination to get himself out of his predicament. Offers of training are turned down and he abandons jobs as soon as he encounters the first obstacle.

Both GPs and counsellors may find it hard to tolerate men like this, and are quite relieved when they do not return. Apathy and passivity, both expressions of unconscious hostility, are difficult to engage with. There is little ego strength in such patients with which to make an alliance. Their feelings are so bleak that they see no point in making plans or carrying them through to a satisfactory conclusion. In turn their professional carers see no point in offering treatment. 'Perfect care' seems far away, and hopeless patients evoke hopelessness in their carers.

A new way forward

We have already suggested that GPs who employ counsellors in their practices may feel disillusioned with a purely scientific approach to the treatment of physical illness, and as they become increasingly unable to perform the counselling role themselves they welcome the contribution of a counsellor to deepen their understanding of their relationships with patients. In the past it was usual for GPs to refer patients with psychological difficulties to specialist psychotherapy clinics, and the level of communication between these services and the GP was usually in the form of a letter from the specialist clinic after the patient had been assessed. Treatment itself, when it was offered and taken up, was long and given under conditions of strict confidentiality, so that GPs often did not know what was happening to their patients. On the whole the relationship between doctor and the psychotherapy clinic was distant, formal and fragmented. By offering counsellors on-site space, GPs saw a way of retaining indirect control of supplementary treatment.

Advantages of counsellor attachments

Advantages for the patient

One direct advantage of counsellor attachments for patients is that it enables them to be seen on site for diagnostic assessment and short-term help. Indirectly, counsellor attachments mean that regular and informed discussions can take place between doctors and counsellors for the good of the patient. This is considered a helpful means of improving the quality of care available.

Advantages for the GP

Apart from the obvious advantages of having a counsellor as part of the primary care team, GPs have reported benefits to themselves. It can be comforting to discuss professional and organisational difficulties with an outsider, and new perspectives can prove enlightening. An experienced counsellor will recognise the full force of the desperation, disturbance and pain that patients project onto their doctors. A doctor may choose to discuss with a trusted counsellor the effects of patients' life events, their histories of deprivation and/or abuse and the effects of this on their personality development.

Advantages for the counsellor

For the counsellor, attachment to a practice provides the opportunity to experience first-hand the pressures, time frames and purposes of the work, in contrast to the more ordered and formal shape of specialist psychotherapy services or private practice. Counsellors are forced to rethink learned models of work and the length of time and intensity of sessions within which the work is done. Counsellors discover the differences between the ideals set in the training environment and the reality of work on the ground. In primary care, counselling is likely to be more focused, curtailed and rapid (see Chapter 1).

First steps

The counsellor as stranger

As newcomers, counsellors have to reflect on their own presence in the surgery and the impact that their arrival will have on relationships within the team. These reflections need to include the counsellor's own state of mind. In the first instance the counsellor is likely to experience *stranger anxiety*. The primary care situation will be suffused with strangeness and it will take time for the counsellor's relationship with the doctors to become established. Stranger anxiety may also be felt by doctors, whose own fantasies and expectations are challenged by the proximity of the counsellor.

Logistically, arrangements have to be specifically tailored to the needs of the counsellor, such as suitable accommodation, furniture and the restriction of interruptions, including telephone calls. Doctors and counsellors will want to discuss how to tell patients about the availability of counselling, how appointments can be made and how cancellations and subsequent appointments will be handled. The issue of interruptions is crucial. The culture of primary care allows for, and anticipates, regular interruptions during consultations, but it is part of the counselling culture to avoid all interruptions except in dire emergencies. Other disciplines may not understand the reasons for these boundaries in counselling work.

Testing each other out

Although the culture has changed since the 1970s, in our experience almost every time a new attachment of a counsellor to the primary care team begins, the wheel has to be reinvented. There is bound to be an initial period of testing the new boundaries. By this we mean that whatever agreements have been reached in the abstract, doctors and counsellors embarking on a real relationship have to redefine their aims, their expectations of each other and their differences as they go along and try to develop a common language. In spite of the different time frames within which each discipline operates, doctor and counsellor have to learn to work in tandem. For instance it is not uncommon for newly appointed counsellors to be faced with a referral list of so-called 'impossible cases', who have previously been referred to other specialists or have long psychiatric histories and very few internal resources to cope with life. Such an introduction is meant to convey to the arriving counsellor something of the long-standing difficulties the GPs have had to cope with single-handedly. It could also be seen as a plea for urgent help in dealing with cases that hitherto have been contained rather precariously. The doctor–counsellor relationship has to survive a tough period of initiation.

The developing relationship

GPs and counsellors need to map out general guidelines about their relationship, so that each may develop mutually comfortable ways of relating. A counsellor working with a team of several doctors may develop different ways of relating to each doctor, including the possibility that in some cases a relationship will be impossible.

Communication with individual GPs

Counsellors and doctors may have different ideas about the frequency and amount of time devoted to pre- and post-referral discussions about patients. Methods of communication will vary and may include written memos, letters, computer data, verbal exchanges or in some cases no communication at all. Some counsellors prefer to have formal letters from referring GPs; others are content to accept all new referrals without prior discussion. Generally, communications operate somewhere between these two poles.

Post-referral discussions also vary. Some counsellors expect to have regular feed-back discussions with the referring GPs and to be involved in joint planning. Counsellors and GPs who have little or no post-referral discussion or communication work fairly independently, usually using the medical notes or computers as the means of exchanging information.

Individual GPs and counsellors may arrange to have informal meetings, say at the end of surgery time when it is quieter, to discuss several patients seen by the counsellor that week. Sometimes GPs and counsellors may never find a fixed time for discussions, but seize whatever time is available between patients during surgery hours.

Teamwork

While relationships with individual GPs are important, the counsellor's collective relationships also matter. The counsellor will want to link up with existing networks in the practice. Are there team meetings? Who attends? Will the counsellor be included? What is discussed at the meetings? Does discussion of cases focus on practical management, or is there also a clinical element to the discussion, where one or two cases are looked at in detail? Are the team meetings attended by the same people every time, or just occasionally when they are available? In some attachments it is common for doctors to have separate meetings with the mental health staff, the administrative staff and the physical therapies staff, as well as meetings among themselves.

A learning process

While there are many ways for GPs and counsellors to organise their meetings, we believe it is essential to establish certain basic principles.

The first principle concerns the establishment and maintenance of the highest possible standards of direct *professional service* to patients, which can best be achieved by open, regular and honest discussions between doctors and counsellors based on a relationship of equality. This implies that everyone in the caring enterprise in primary care should work towards protecting a mutually agreed space in which formal and informal discussions about patients can take place.

Second, whatever the service requirements for counselling in primary care, and whatever the cost factors, all those involved with the GP–counsellor attachment should recognise that they are engaged in a *learning process*. When the attachment makes a positive and valued contribution to primary health provision, doctors may begin to see an added and beneficial dimension to their work, an unfolding of their vision of what treatment can bring.

As for the counsellors, there is a direct challenge to the measured pace of treatment so often regarded as the model for counselling. Here counsellors have to make a rapid connection between the body and the mind, while allowing patients to make those connections at their own speed. Overall their professional identity, their understanding of illness and significantly, their relationships with their patients are influenced by the proximity of medical doctors. GPs may claim that they do not want to know about their patients' psychological world, and counsellors may be suspicious of orthodox medical models, but over time each is likely to see the advantages of the other's approach, and find that they are influenced by them. Without recommending that counsellors change into doctors, or doctors into counsellors, we believe this is a good thing. Inevitably counsellors learn about and become alert to the medical needs of their patients and refer patients back to their GPs for medication or hospitalisation. In turn GPs learn about counselling and utilise the knowledge gained from counsellors regarding the unconscious meanings of symptoms and illness and how these are used in family relationships and in patients' communications with their doctors (see the examples in Chapter 8 on key professional issues, and Chapter 7 on psychosomatic illness).

CASE EXAMPLE: THE TRAINEE GP

In a meeting between two GPs, their trainee and two practice counsellors, the trainee GP wonders when it might be appropriate to refer a patient to a counsellor, and when that moment arrives, how the subject of referral should be broached. The trainee GP says he feels anxious about making referrals in case the patient might feel that:

1. The GP does not know what to do next.
2. The doctor is washing his hands of him.

3. He is 'too much' for the doctor to handle.
4. He has a 'serious' problem.
5. He might be mad.
6. He will be very angry having to start all over again with someone new.

When discussing this issue it emerges that each of the two GPs has a different view about referrals, and significantly their feelings about referral touch on their own identity as doctors. One says that he is loath to broach any subject with patients that could lead to an 'opening up' of feelings in case he is detained for more than ten minutes. This GP acknowledges that it is not the ten minutes that worries him, but rather that he has a distinct dislike of 'feelings' as he is a practical, medical person seeking answers to technical medical problems. 'Feelings' are a matter for the counsellor. He explains to patients that the counsellors will 'deal with' their problems. At one level this GP perceives counsellors in his own image – applying technical solutions to human problems in much the same way that he does to medical problems. The second GP prefers to extend her counselling time with patients for as long as possible, enjoying the experience of a more intimate exploration of difficulties. She refers patients to counsellors on the basis that she thinks it is good for everyone, including GPs, to talk to someone about their problems. She encourages many patients to visit the counsellor for a chat, and in so doing helps to remove the mystique surrounding counselling.

It is difficult to determine what the GP trainee made of these two very different ways of attending to the mental health needs of patients in primary care. He said he was not sure whether to believe that depression was organic or psychological, a good or a bad thing; whether he should prescribe or refer, or in which order he should do this. There is no short answer to these questions and GPs may have to arrive at a view that reflects their own beliefs. Nevertheless the trainee's question seems to reflect broader issues surrounding the underlying philosophy and values in the practice team about the part that social and family factors play in the cause of physical illness and recovery. It seems that those present at the meeting shared an image of an *ideal* patient with mild, clear and treatable ailments, who was cooperative, intelligent and grateful. Anyone presenting with disturbing, mysterious or intractable problems was treated sympathetically, but was nevertheless unwelcome.

Pondering about the reasons why patients landed in such situations was of little interest to those at the meeting, but the two counsellors' insistence on talking about such patients led to some interesting ideas about their future management. The group began to review traditional models of caring for untreatable, 'heart-sink' patients. Ideas included the possibility of a GP and counsellor seeing patients together; more emphasis on group and family interviews; and the abandonment of the 'treatment–cure' equation for problem families. It was recognised that problem families may hold on to poor family relationships as tenaciously as they cling to childish hopes of transforming them.

This was a good meeting. It was a cornerstone of a change in attitude and practice with problem patients. Something had shifted in the GP–counsellor relationship away from the one-way traffic of referring GP to receiving counsellor, towards greater mutual interdependence (see Chapter 4 on referrals).

Power of relationships

The above example illustrates the harmonious relationship that may evolve between doctors and counsellors if there is enough goodwill on both sides and each understands what the other has to deal with. By working together they may both work better, and in this way a shift may occur from a hierarchical power relationship to a more equal one. Relying on power relationships may be a response to anxious, sometimes desperate situations, but power can also lead to rigidity of personality and closed minds (Guggenbühl-Craig, 1982). Acknowledging differences in others requires a certain humility and can lead to greater openness and a willingness to learn. When patients wish their helpers to be omnipotent, it is easy to fall into line with those wishes and begin to believe that we can provide omnipotent solutions. To be fruitful the GP–counsellor relationship must contain the seeds of hope, have its foundations in mutual respect and function for the benefit of patients.

Rivalry and competition

In sharp contrast to the ideal and evolving GP–counsellor relationships outlined above, we have seen many less healthy alternatives. Some find expression through rivalry, where the two complementary strands of the primary care team compete for 'ownership' of patients, each hoping to become the 'special' one to whom the patients reveal themselves in preference to the other. Both sides may fear encroachment by the other, or feel deskilled by the presence of an expert in a domain in which each has ruled supreme. While GPs generally welcome the presence of a skilled person who can take some difficult patients off their hands, they may feel disgruntled about surrendering aspects of their work that have traditionally belonged to family doctors. It is important for both sides to confront these ambivalent feelings.

CASE EXAMPLE: BEATRICE

Fifty-seven year-old Beatrice tells the counsellor that she is suffering from depression and a collapsed vertebra. Her main concern is the amount of medication she is taking for depression, anxiety and sleep problems. She feels disappointed with herself for relying on medication, and wonders aloud whether her GP has been too 'pill-happy' with her. The way Beatrice talks about her medical care causes the counsellor to feel irritated with the GP, suspecting that he might have referred Beatrice to compensate for his guilt about not paying sufficient attention to what she was really trying to say. This feeling of irritation turns to annoyance when Beatrice reveals that her real fear is breast cancer. She has also become alarmed the previous year when she developed constipation and associated pain. She says she cannot talk to anyone about her fears, including her husband, in case she annoys him. She suspects that she has annoyed her GP, who in response has referred her to the counsellor. While she is pleased to have at last found someone to whom she can talk about her fears of cancer, the referral has in some way reinforced her belief that she has an awful disease that her doctor cannot discuss with her.

The counsellor and patient then go on to discuss the patient's relationship with her doctor, and it is suggested that the counsellor might talk to the GP and prepare the way for him to talk realistically about cancer and the chances of Beatrice having the disease. Beatrice is visibly relieved and declares that she is a 'worrier', just like her mother, and confesses that her nights are seriously disturbed by a growing terror of 'being eaten up' from within. Beatrice is referred back to her GP, who talks to her about her cancer fears and offers her regular breast examinations.

This example illustrates the way a doctor and a counsellor can be put into potentially rivalrous situations by thinking he or she is the one who understands the patient best. In this case the counsellor helpfully refers the patient back to the GP after a good short-term intervention.

Relationships and work style

During the first few months of an attachment GPs and counsellors have to learn how to make and receive referrals (see Chapter 4 on referrals). The counsellor's preferred approach to treatment may form part of this negotiation. It is not uncommon for doctors to perceive treatment as a definite input that will result in a tangible output. In the same way as medication can be measured through certain assessable improvement targets, so too may a fixed counselling input of say six sessions be expected to produce clear results.

We wondered why the figure six is widely regarded as significant by so many authorities in the field (Curtis-Jenkins, 1996). Why has it become a talisman figure, comparable to a fortnight's supply of drugs? We have reached the conclusion that the figure six was identified from a retrospective data survey (Harris and Pringle, 1994) that revealed that the average number of patient visits to the counsellor was six. This also happens to coincide with the average number of patient visits to the GP in any one year. Counsellors themselves usually take a different view of the value and significance of six visits. They believe that working with psychological defences requires more rather than less time and that relationships and dependency feelings need cautious treatment over a longer period. As a result of this preference for a longer, slower encounter, GPs may perceive the patient–counsellor relationship as overcherished and overprotected, which may in turn stir up negative feelings, rivalry and competition and lead to hostility between GPs and counsellors. Doctors often say that they could do this kind of work themselves were it not for the pressure of time and other bureaucratic demands. These statements and positions can be used defensively and lead to the postponement of discussions about the role and purpose of the counsellor attachment.

Relationships: unity or fragmentation

The arrival of a counsellor may be treated by GPs as an opportunity to be rid of problem patients, rather than a chance to engage in joint deliberations, canvas opinions and tease out common strategies for patient care. This tendency imposes a particular burden of responsibility on both GPs and counsellors to find constructive and efficient ways of working together. There may be few precedents to follow. Each professional has to learn about the role, training, background and expectations of the other. It is not uncommon for medical models to predominate as the setting is, after all, a medical one. However there is a place for counselling models. GP and counsellor may contribute uniquely to working with illness, ageing, frailty, loss and death. The challenge in developing this new relationship is whether doctor and counsellor can work together collaboratively as a team, without compromising the unique contributions that each makes to patient care.

Problems in the doctor–counsellor relationship

Some flash-points in the doctor–counsellor relationship are to be expected; jealousy and battles for control are almost inevitable. It is our contention that if these conflicts are not dealt with professionally and seriously through dialogue, problems may develop and the relationship will become toxic. A potential source of difficulty lies in the nature of the contact that patients have with their GPs and counsellors. Following a counselling session, it is not uncommon for patients to have an appointment with their doctor for medical purposes, and to use this as an opportunity to discuss their feelings about the session with the counsellor. This may undermine the work of the counsellor, particularly if it goes unreported. Counsellors may be further undermined if the doctor pursues an independent line of action, such as prescribing medication for depression without discussing it first.

This situation suggests that two different processes are operating in primary care: the 'politics of salvation' and the 'politics of revelation' (Lawrence, 1994) (see also Appendix A). In the politics of salvation, patients and their doctors are engaged in a process that aims to reduce, or preferably remove, patients' anxieties about the deterioration of their bodies. Counselling, on the other hand, is engaged in the politics of revelation, as it aims to reveal aspects of the patients' emotional and psychological world through discussion that helps them gain deeper insights into their ways of functioning. Of course not all patients want insight, and one reason why they are seeing the counsellor may be their GP's impatience, irritation or despair with them. The possession of these feelings by the GP often cannot be acknowledged, but instead are wrapped up and disguised as a referral to the counsellor. The nature of the developing relationship between counsellor and GP may be better understood by examining the type of patient who is referred, the underlying reason for the referral and why it is taking place at that particular moment. Unconscious forces at work in the GP–counsellor relationship can be a useful source of information about the patient's mental state if the GP and counsellor are alert to them at the time of referral (see Chapter 4 on referrals).

This book emphasises that without an understanding of the unconscious components that exist in all relationships the primary care team will operate at less than efficient levels. We believe that unconscious elements operate most forcefully in conditions of severe anxiety, particularly about health issues that are coupled with expectations of a 'magical cure'. Magic has long been associated with medicine and doctors. We all hope that doctors will take away our pain, remove our illnesses and even prevent our death. In many situations, of course, doctors do facilitate dramatic improvements. Medicine now has powerful remedies at its disposal for the treatment of ailments that in previous ages were accepted fatalistically. However it is also true that neither medicine, the health service nor any of its officials can postpone mortality indefinitely. Sensitive ways have to be found for doctors and counsellors to help patients come to terms with their fantasies of medical infallibility. We firmly believe that doctors and counsellors can work well together in a framework of humane sensitive acknowledgement and acceptance of patients' anxieties.

GPs and counsellors may find themselves enacting any one of a number of different, all-embracing, defensive roles in the practice as a way of managing internal or external conflict or pressures, as follows:

GP defence strategies

- *The robot* deals with internal and external pressures in a mechanistic, often ordered and obsessional way.
- *The saviour* tries to do everything for patients and staff in the practice, thereby avoiding helplessness and disappointment.
- *The dictator* uses authority and control as a way of managing anxiety and uncertainty.
- *The iceberg* distances him/herself from painful emotional situations and conflicts and may retreat into the medicalisation of problems.

Counsellor defence strategies

- *The saviour*, like the GP, tries to rescue anyone and everyone in distress and may overestimate his/her capacities
- *The mother* provides space, warmth and care, in contrast to the harassed, busy GP
- *The dustbin* accepts all referrals, however inappropriate, as an unconscious means of relieving the GP of the anxiety aroused by difficult patients.
- *The slave* perceives that he or she must be subservient to the medical practitioners in the practice and cannot fight for 'equal' rights in creating a satisfying job.
- *The rival* may see him/herself to be in competition with the GPs or other practice staff in terms of responsibility for patients, methods of work, 'right' answers and so on.

Finally, professionals in primary care may deal with their frustrations and ambivalent feelings about patients by making disparaging remarks about patients behind their backs. A counsellor who is aware of the dynamic processes in institutions may be able to help staff to think about this type of 'split', where one face is presented to the patient and another to professional colleagues. The opportunity to discuss feelings about patients can lead to improved care and also boost morale at work. Splitting produces relief in the short term, but brings long-term demoralisation.

Professional identity and teamwork

What does a counsellor do that is distinctive? Phrases such as 'counselling is a unique combination of intimacy and distance in a relationship', 'struggling together' or 'using the self in the service of another' do not provide a sufficient definition of counselling in primary care that can satisfy outsiders.

The following factors contribute to a professional sense of identity.

Knowledge, not action, as a contribution to identity

Professional identity is usually defined by what we do. Solicitors advocate, engineers design and build, teachers teach. Their activities are easily comprehended by the public. It is assumed that their activities, the things they do and the skills they require to do them, have been acquired through a formal programme of training and that there are professional bodies to oversee their standards and ethics. Counselling is another matter. Counselling does not constitute a visible activity that can be easily described, emulated or measured. The identity of counsellors derives instead from possession of a particular understanding about the inner world of mind, identity, feelings and relationships, and the methods employed by individuals, their families, partners, friends and groups to sustain themselves in the face of conflict.

Counsellors also know how to convey that understanding in their interviews as instruments for positive life changes. Apart from arranging appointments, securing the physical environment, listening, attending, empathising, interpreting and explaining, the counsellor does not *do* much. We have to conclude that counsellors' identity is based on their unique understanding and knowledge of people and the methods employed to make that knowledge available to others. This knowledge is partly theory- based and partly research-based, but it is also 'soft' knowledge, open to different interpretations that may vary according to the counsellor's experiences and views. In other words, counsellors may be open to charges of vagueness.

Attitude as a contribution to identity

The counsellor's identity is also influenced by the fact that patients have the right to make their own decisions, however imperfectly, and that full knowledge of any patient is impossible. Counsellors' attitudes are necessarily characterised by humility combined with strength of conviction about key issues. These include the importance of boundaries, the presence of both constructive and destructive forces in every situation, the presence of lateral rather than linear thinking in affairs of the mind and the influence of role on behaviour. Role issues are no less crucial to the development of the counsellor's own identity in the primary care team, which brings us back to the question of what makes the counsellor's contribution unique among the primary care disciplines.

Counsellors rarely use the word 'healing' to describe their activities because of its association with illness and a reluctance to be perceived as possessing 'cures'. They prefer to construct their own identity on the assumption that there is a 'healer' within every patient and they only have to trigger this 'inner healer'. These issues have bedevilled the profession and are likely to continue to do so for some time. Identity issues come to the fore as soon as counsellors begin to face the challenge of joining and becoming members of the multidisciplinary primary care team. Even established counsellors need to communicate their role and function regularly, so that they are clearly understood by colleagues in other disciplines. To their surprise, counsellors and doctors have discovered that they do occasionally become enamoured with each other's roles, tasks and status. Some even yearn to be in the other's position, and if a role reversal should take place, either consciously or unconsciously, unexpected and not always helpful consequences can result.

CASE EXAMPLE: SWAPPING ROLES

In one attachment the GP and counsellor become so immersed in the psychodynamics of a patient that the counsellor omits to ask how she is currently supporting herself financially, while the GP overlooks the possibility of psychiatric illness that might require medication. The situation comes to a head when the counsellor finds himself pressing the GP to prescribe antidepressants. The GP responds with: 'hold on a minute, I thought this was supposed to be my job'. Both professionals are then forced to look hard at what has happened to their roles, and why they have allowed themselves to be seduced away from them. They conclude that the rivalry that often characterises GP–counsellor roles has a flip side of mutual admiration and emulation (benign envy). Professional identity is supposed to help practitioners in their roles, but when there are different, but overlapping identities, either friction or fusion may result.

Identity and status

There are undeniable status differences between doctors and counsellors. Counselling, although important as an effective and supportive component of patient care, plays a secondary role. In many cases its impact is slow and marginal. Counsellors often lack confidence, are poorly paid and, unlike their medical colleagues, do not have dramatic and immediate effects on their patients. In contrast to doctors, their identity can be fragile, porous and indeterminate, making them hesitant and isolated team members. They are often lone practitioners without collegial support on site, relying instead on outside support groups to provide reassurance, comfort, nourishment and reinforcement of their professional identity. Some support groups of primary care counsellors tend to emphasise the counsellors' 'sameness' and lodge all 'difference' outside, in the practice team.

Positive identity

Counselling is now a distinct discipline with many different styles, and counsellors are aware of different approaches to suit the needs of different patients. When counsellors see patients for an initial assessment they become both diagnostician and provider, although in other cases their knowledge of local psychotherapeutic resources may lead them to refer outwards to a service provider.

The identity of counsellors is formed and influenced by their core discipline, their original training and any subsequent training they may undertake. The content and nature of their work, who employs them, the amount of time they spend in the surgery and the nature of the relationship they develop with the GPs also contributes to their sense of who they are.

Negative identity

Counsellors' identity can be said to be defensive, placing emphasis on what they do *not do* rather than on what they *do*. For example counsellors are heard to declare proudly that they do not give advice, are not directive and are not judgemental. On the other hand, many of the things they do are also components of the roles of other members of the practice team: they listen, they empathise, they think, they speak. It is therefore not surprising, that counsellors have problems with their own identity and integration into the primary care team while also remaining distinct. Counselling is currently grappling with these identity issues by seriously questioning assumptions and seeking ways to adapt its skills to the pressures and demands of the work.

Subsequent training

Professional identity based on the counsellor's original training experience is easy to describe. Some counsellors have moved into counselling work from a core discipline of psychiatry, psychology, social work or nursing, whereas others have no core discipline but have trained as counsellors on the strength of a relevant degree and work experience. All have become specialists by combining their understanding of the inner world of feelings and emotions with the outer world realities of personal and family relationships, work and social institutions. For counsellors who are trained psychotherapists and psychoanalysts, the challenge of the work lies in the application of psychoanalytic thinking to the counselling relationship in a busy general practice, seeing a significant number of patients for assessment and a few for short-term counselling. Their work could not be described as psychotherapy or psychoanalysis, but many use a psychoanalytic frame of reference in all aspects of their work, making fruitful use of concepts that include the unconscious, defences, ambivalence, denial and internal conflict (see Appendix A).

Summary

In this chapter we have described the factors, both positive and negative, that influence the doctor–counsellor relationship. We have suggested ways of managing the difficulties that are encountered when a newcomer, the counsellor, enters an existing organisation with established patterns of relationships and ways of doing things. Each participant in the enterprise has expectations of the newcomer, and it is up to the counsellor to help define his or her identity by entering into dialogue with all members of the team. It is likely that the newcomer will be imbued with hope that old or intractable problems will be resolved.

The point made to us repeatedly is that ongoing dialogue is a necessary part of team building and good care of patients. An underlying aim of teamwork in primary care is to bring together the body and mind, psyche and soma. This forms the basis of a unifying principle of integration in a health service that is noted for its tendency to separate things from each other. We write from the position that individuals and systems move between integration and separation in order to deal with anxiety about themselves and the work they do. Hence some practitioners prefer to work alone and are clear about the limits of what they are able to achieve, while others prefer to work in teams and see themselves as contributing to the professional work of other disciplines.

The impetus to work together has come from changing circumstances and new attitudes in society. Pressures towards fragmentation in primary care have been matched by the desire to create effective collaborating teams that will have benefits for patients, doctors and counsellors. Maintaining good relationships, a professional identity, effective communication, teamwork and learning are all vital aspects of the new partnership between doctors and counsellors. Each aspect needs to be carefully considered in every partnership at its inception and reviewed as it progresses.

3

THE NATURE OF THE WORK

Philosophies of work

Throughout history the two-person relationship (pairs/partners) has been at the root of the total gratification fantasy. We only have to look at fantasies of the mother–baby relationship, or religious beliefs about man's dependency relationship with God, to see evidence of the wish for permanent relief from pain. The two most basic and predominant assumptions operating in health care organisations are about dependency and pairing. Although in certain circumstances these basic assumptions can interfere with task performance, they can be useful in the functioning of specific types of professional activity, such as medicine and counselling. At the heart of the dependency notion is the belief that security and protection are attainable from one individual, as expressed, for example, in the meeting between patient and doctor or patient and counsellor. Patients arrive seeking help – literally helpless with insufficient knowledge to solve their own problems – and feeling inadequate. Their weak and dependent behaviour implies that in contrast doctors and counsellors are powerful and knowledgeable. In this emotional state the patient demands that all explanations are kept extremely simple; he or she cannot understand any complexity nor undertake anything difficult. Only the carer has the ability to put all difficulties right. This idealisation of the carer transforms him or her into an all-encompassing figure. When a dependent patient feels that life is cold and unfriendly, the carer offers a temporary sense of comfort and security.

In Bion's (1961) pairing theory, the patient's demeanour offers the carer a heightened significance and influence, status and adulation that are expected to result in benefits on both sides. Their pairing contains the spirit of hopefulness. Not much needs to be done. Just being there is sufficient. The pair live in the hope of creating a new state of being, sowing the seeds of new optimism. The feelings that surround such pairings are soft, agreeable and simplistic. There is no room here for despair, destructiveness or hate.

For the professionals, the motivations underpinning work, like other aspects of human activity, have their roots in the deepest and most primitive levels of the mind. The intensity and complexity of doctors' and counsellors' feelings about their roles are attributable to those situations that evoke early infantile memories and their accompanying emotions. Medicine and counselling are both associated with restorative drives that stem from the wish to repair 'internal damaged objects' by applying remedies to real external physical illness or damaged patients. These ideas about the influence of unconscious processes on work derive from the theories of Freud, particularly as developed and elaborated by Melanie Klein (Klein, 1952, 1975). It is not uncommon for people to deal with anxieties about their aggression by selecting a profession that offers them opportunities to 'heal' their damaged or dead 'inner objects' by attending to the needs of others who are damaged or injured. This unconscious drive to 'repair' often lies behind the career choice of both doctors and counsellors.

Adapting to primary health care

Duration of counselling

Controversy surrounds the question of whether all cases should be seen for a fixed number of sessions, or whether, in the style of traditional counselling and psychotherapy, patients should be seen for an indefinite number of sessions as long as the clinical justification remains. Should the model of work be open-ended and flexible to allow a free associative process to govern the length and pace of the counselling relationship? Or should all patients be given a fixed, rationed number of strictly focused sessions, no matter what their needs are? Some contend that working to a fixed number of sessions does not allow the relationship with the patient to develop properly. On the other hand, 'developing the relationship' may not be the main task of primary-care-based counselling. We hold that the model of counselling appropriate to this setting should resemble, in at least some respects, the general aims and characteristics of primary care, namely to provide an adequate minimum level of health care to the greatest number of people. Service providers with limited resources will always have to contend with the difficulty of large numbers of patients with varying degrees of medical, emotional and psychological need. While a preliminary sifting of patients suitable for counselling will be carried out by the referring GP, the counsellor, as part of a multidisciplinary team, will bear some responsibility for the fair allocation of available therapeutic resources. This means that, difficult as it is, counsellors will become part of the process of determining who gets what and how much of their clinical input.

Coexistence and shared values

It is inevitable that when one discipline, such as counselling, operates within a larger system, such as primary care, the smaller system will eventually come to resemble the larger. If not, discord will corrode their coexistence until the smaller system is either suppressed or extruded from the larger. Common values can make the partnership durable. Minimalism is part of the nature of primary care with the clinician asking her- or himself: 'What is the most expedient way of reaching a reasonable solution?' rather than: 'What are the ideal methods of bringing about an optimal solution?'

Addressing psychological defences

The question remains as to whether the counsellor should be dealing with patients' psychological defences in primary care at all. If time is scarce, which defences should receive attention and which should be ignored? The main justification for employing counsellors is the belief that patients will benefit from talking to a professional about their worries, illnesses, families and life problems. But work in primary care is all about limits, and both GP and counsellor have to work within that reality. For the counsellor, this may mean adapting those time-intensive models and philosophies of counselling that were formed during training, such as working gently at the patient's pace, respecting the nature of and reasons for psychological defences, especially denial, resistance, narcissism and idealisation. Working within a psychodynamic framework, with its emphasis on interpreting defences against anxiety and protecting the individual from feelings of shame and guilt, can take up much time in private psychotherapy before any change in the patient's symptoms or personality becomes obvious. The slower pace dictated by the needs of patients in counselling can jar with the more rapid approach to problem solving in medicine.

Additional training

Counsellors and psychotherapists believe that talking helps but that specialist training in the 'talking cure' is a prerequisite. Illness, disability and loneliness, deterioration and ultimately death, in their view, all evoke particular defences that have to be handled with exceptional sensitivity if the patient is not to be made to feel bad, or worse still, damaged. Conversely it is well known that certain defences are associated with particular illnesses. For example repression of anger is connected with respiratory diseases and excessive anxiety with disturbances of the gastrointestinal tract (see Chapter 7 on psychosomatic illness). Such interdependence of psychological defences with illness demands that counsellors undertake extensive training in the psychological, emotional and biological bases of personality development. Specialist clinical experience in a hospital or other medical setting is desirable, as is a reasonable period of personal counselling or psychotherapy in order to learn about personal feelings and defences. Good supervision is essential.

What do patients expect from the counsellor?

During a consultation with the GP, patients may convey something about themselves, some clue to their 'inner world' or mental state that prompts the GP to offer access to a counsellor. This may be the first time that the patient has considered engaging in a professional conversation with someone other than their doctor. Will the GP push it or leave it? Only a small number of patients request a referral. This may happen in areas where people are familiar and open to the concept of talking as a means of resolving personal problems. In GP-led initiatives, patients may welcome the suggestion, fear it, or even reject the offer. Whatever their reactions, apart from some vague ideas about the nature of counselling, patients are unlikely to know what will happen to them when they see the counsellor, what kind of questions the counsellor will ask and how much of themselves they will be obliged to reveal. Will the conversations remain confidential? How many sessions of counselling will they be offered? Must they make a commitment at the outset? Patients may wonder whether the method will be cognitive, behavioural, psychodynamic, systemic or supportive. All these questions will cross the new patient's mind and may add to his or her hesitation about embarking on this course of action.

The doctor, as employer and head of the clinical team, engages professional staff to extend the range of care available to her or his patients, and therefore counsellors attend to patients *on behalf of* the patient's doctor. Both counsellor and patient need to know this at the outset, so that all parties are aware that discussions between doctor and counsellor will take place. While the relationship between doctor and patient and between counsellor and patient appears to be distinctly two-way, they share a three-way link. Our understanding of the two-way relationship rests on the paradigm of nursing mother and baby, a pair whose basic needs are exquisitely met. This early relationship forms the basis of the projected fantasy, discussed already, that the doctor will satisfy all the patient's basic needs; with the arrival of the counsellor a three-person relationship is established, an oedipal one, containing all the elements of competition and rivalry, jealousy and retribution for secret and forbidden desires that may be known to and disapproved of by the absent 'other' carer. A benign way of looking at this scenario involves good communication between doctor and counsellor and represents a resolution of the child/patient's oedipal struggle, resulting in the sense of security and tranquillity that comes from collaborating parents/carers. From this it should be clear that neither the doctor nor the counsellor need feel impelled to provide total solutions for their patients. If they can truly collaborate, using and appreciating each other's skills, then they may discover outcomes that neither of them could attain alone.

Once a counsellor joins the primary care team a new range of possibilities is opened up. One immediate benefit is the opportunity to offer help to patients on the premises rather than at specialist clinics. External referral can often sow the seeds of anxiety in a patient's mind: 'is my problem so serious that I need to attend a psychiatric clinic?' Moreover the existence of a counsellor in the practice means that a greater number of problems can be addressed earlier, 'nipping them in the bud' as it were, and many patients feel more comfortable at their local health centre, an accessible, local and familiar place.

Skills of the counsellor

Psychodynamics lie at the heart of counselling. Yet to be effective, counsellors must command a broad range of skills; without them they will be unable fully to address their patients' needs. For instance some counsellors may not have been trained in cognitive analytical therapy or stress management, but these techniques may be just what the patient requires. A team of practice counsellors should ideally cover the whole range between them. Some practices employ counsellors and psychologists in order that each may complement the skills of the other. Counsellors and psychologists stand to gain from one another by having complementary skills. Psychologists are usually trained in stress management and cognitive analytic therapy and many patients in primary care require that style of approach. There is little danger of rivalry and competition among counsellors working together when each uses a distinctive approach. In addition, anxieties about not being regarded as sufficiently well-trained are reduced when working alongside someone who has supplementary skills. Their range of different skills makes it easier for GPs to match patients' needs with counsellors' expertise. In cases where just one psychodynamically oriented counsellor covers all the practice needs, some in-service training in other approaches will be beneficial.

Therapeutic modalities

Counsellors' approach to the work is influenced by their theoretical orientation, ideas on personality development and identity, the nature of the presenting problem and the limitations of time and other resources. Under pressure, the counsellor might have to blend a range of approaches such as psychodynamic with behavioural in some cases, or a combination of supportive and cognitive in others. In this book we argue that in the provision of counselling and other mental health services, the team should ideally comprise the broadest possible range of orientations and modalities. By modalities we mean the different types of counselling interventions, assessment, short- and long-term individual therapy, couple therapy, family and group therapy. This covers the widest possible spectrum. We must also take account of the range of patients with whom counsellors work: children, adolescents, mothers, middle-aged people, the elderly, the physically ill, the psychiatrically ill, HIV patients, and so on. However it can be difficult to introduce the full range of counselling modalities into the surgery because patients are linked into wider social networks in and around the practice. For instance patients may be reluctant to participate in group therapy if they are likely to meet other participants in the neighbourhood, or they may expect or prefer a more traditional one-to-one approach. Patients visit their doctors as individuals unless they are children brought by their parents. Patients visit the practice nurse as individuals. To introduce the idea of people coming together as couples for couples therapy, with their children for family therapy or to join with strangers for group therapy is a new and often daunting idea. The benefits seem neither obvious nor acceptable to most people.

The counsellor as generalist or specialist

It is quite common these days to find all types of counsellor working in a practice, including crisis counsellors, bereavement counsellors, HIV counsellors and renal counsellors. Patients in primary care require counsellors to be both generalists and specialists. Pietroni sums up this dilemma:

> Although the referrals individually did not go beyond my expectations in terms of range of presenting problems, seriousness of disturbance and range of social class and situation, collectively they did. I could feel in no uncertain terms the impact of general practice: the complex switches from one problem to another without respite in between, the dramatically different needs of the patients and expectations from the referrer (Pietroni, 1995, p. 454).

Pietroni demonstrates that the counsellor in primary care is a 'specialist kind of generalist', because the area of work is specialised in the very broadest sense, to cover the fullest range of psychological, emotional and relationship difficulties – physical and psychiatric illness, poor or violent childhoods, traumatic events, dislocation and upheaval of all kinds – the consequences of which appear in the doctor's surgery on a daily basis. Generalist and specialist skills are required because the counsellor conducts many first-time assessments with patients without any prior knowledge of their situation. While much of the counsellor's own work is specialised, a referring counsellor, rerouting patients after a single assessment interview, gives the work a generalist character.

CASE EXAMPLE: GILL

Gill, a 25 year old single woman, complains of being obsessed with hostile thoughts towards strangers in the street. She is worried about these because they are so out of character with her normal, caring sensitive personality. It emerges in the course of her initial meeting with the counsellor that she has a younger brother who has been diagnosed as schizophrenic. Her main worry is that she too might be losing her mind and it appears that Gill is seeking reassurance about her mental state. After taking a thorough personal and family history, it emerges that her anxiety is a reaction to the significant dislocations in her life over the past year. Once the causes are understood, reassurance follows and Gill feels greatly relieved. She is offered another appointment a month later. The intervention seems to have been sufficient but the door has been left open for further exploration, so that her situation can be reviewed and another course of action taken, if necessary.

Gill's case demonstrates the generalist/specialist nature of the counselling role. The first step is to contain the patient's anxiety, and once this has been done, work with the patient has already begun. That first interview was essentially an assessment, but in fact it helped in the short term and prepared the ground for further work. We believe that counsellors in partnership with GPs play a key role in the containment of anxiety in primary care. In different circumstances, or in the era before counsellor attachments, the patient may have been referred to the local psychiatric out-patient department. There is good reason to suppose that had this happened to Gill, her anxieties would have escalated rather than diminished. A professional versed in the dynamics of psychiatric illness and psychological processes on site at the local health centre has great value in calming human problems soon after their inception, before they spin out of control.

The employment contract

In some cases the formal employment of counsellors is agreed jointly by the counsellor and the employing doctor, although in many cases the Family Health Service Authority is party to drafting contracts and paying fees. In the past, doctors who were interested in counselling services for their patients consulted with friends in order to find a counsellor who they believed might 'fit in', usually someone already known to them, who demonstrated a flair for the work and had a pleasant disposition. The person may or may not have had any formal counselling training.

While this approach used to be considered acceptable, now that counselling services in primary care have expanded there is much more concern about standards of training and codes of ethics. Codes of practice have been formulated, registers drawn up and a complete disciplinary machinery is in place. The whole enterprise of counselling in primary care is now on a far more formalised footing. Employers pay close attention to the type of training and preparation counsellors have received and the range of skills they can offer the surgery's patients. Salaries are now more standardised, although wide variation between employers can still be found. Counselling has become professionalised and counsellors have become more adept at articulating how their activities should be defined, monitored and rewarded. Counsellors must continue to probe and carve out definitions for the roles they play. This is not a simple matter as their activities are not easily measured for effectiveness (see Chapter 9 on the evaluation of research). Much of what they do seems vague and talking is an activity we all take for granted. However 'professional' conversations are distinct and counsellors have fine-tuned therapeutic talking into their métier. While counselling draws on psychoanalysis, psychotherapy, psychology and social work for its theoretical base, it has also refined and transformed this knowledge sufficiently for a larger slice of the population to benefit from its combined therapies.

Practical requirements

Certain practical needs have to be met for counselling to become a viable enterprise. The first important consideration is privacy and confidentiality. Patients talk to counsellors about very intimate aspects of themselves and these discussions can make them feel anxious, sad, embarrassed or angry. They may never have spoken to anyone about the topics covered with their counsellors. For this reason the creation of a suitable physical environment has to be given very careful attention. The surroundings must feel secure, without interruptions from people entering the room or telephones ringing. The patient must know that the period spent in the room is his or hers exclusively and that the counsellor will devote full attention to them alone.

Reception staff play an important part in easing patients into counselling. They know that counselling patients are seen by appointment and if patients arrive early, the counsellor's work with other patients must not be interrupted to let them know this. In some surgeries counselling patients are directed to separate waiting rooms, so that patients in the general waiting area do not notice when they are collected by the counsellor. Reception staff may need coaching on how to talk to counselling patients: to avoid talking to them about the details of their counselling, to encourage patients who call to cancel their appointments to keep them, or at least to talk to the counsellor before cancelling.

Counsellors have different arrangements for making appointments with patients. In some cases, particularly where computers are used, initial appointments may be made directly by the doctors, who, having consulted the computer, establish that the counsellor has a vacancy. In other cases it is the practice for referrals to be made in writing, whereupon the counsellor, having decided to proceed with an assessment interview, sends the patient an appointment. Other counsellors prefer patients to make their own appointments.

Cancelled or failed appointments are a waste of resources. These may occur because of patient ambivalence about counselling or because of cavalier attitudes towards appointment keeping, a characteristic of primary care. One way round this problem is to send written reminders to new patients a week before their appointments. These reminders stress the difference for patients between spontaneous visits to their GP and attending the surgery at a time specifically set aside for them.

Keeping statistics is necessary and this too involves making arrangements with the receptionists and practice manager.

Time management

Counselling is bound by the clock. The way counsellors operate their service in primary care depends on the number of hours per week the counsellor works in the practice. Attachments of seven hours or fewer mean that counsellors will spend most of their time assessing new patients, sometimes involving difficult treatment decisions. Clearly, in a seven-hour week the counsellor is not able to assess and treat a significant number of patients. Fewer working hours puts pressure on counsellors to work rapidly in short bursts while seeing as great a number of patients as possible. When counsellors work more than seven hours a week they are usually able to divide their time between new assessments and a moderate amount of counselling. Their treatment services include both short-term work and in-depth, longer-term counselling (see Chapter 5 on assessment and treatment options).

GPs can pace themselves according to the number of people waiting to see them, but there are many ways in which a counsellor's time can be allocated. Interviews may last for anything between thirty and sixty minutes, with assessment interviews running for longer. Interviews with couples usually last about sixty minutes and with individuals about fifty minutes. Group sessions usually last between seventy-five and ninety minutes. Occasionally, when patients do not turn up for their appointments the counsellor may agree to see other patients in those slots, so as not to waste time.

Use of time may cause friction between members of the team, particularly between doctor and counsellor. On average doctors see patients every seven to ten minutes, in consultations that are not always planned in advance. They usually occur in response to the sudden onset of illness or need. Flexible time management and availability are the catchwords for work methods in the surgery, although the problem of irritable patients having to wait for long periods in the waiting room is well-documented. In contrast the counsellor's use of time may seem inflexible. Appointments are agreed well in advance and because counsellors work punctually their patients usually arrive on time for their sessions and do not have to wait at all.

When counselling patients are late for their sessions, their late arrival is usually discussed in terms of any unconscious communications the patient may be making to the counsellor. This process is probably alien to doctors and lateness is seldom considered by them, except through patients' complaints. Both patients and doctors operate within a GP appointment system that is open to abuse. Some patients probably take the view that when an appointment to see the doctor is made in advance, non-attendance will not matter since scores of others will be waiting to take their place. The difficulty of operating a structured appointment system in a turn-up-and-be-seen context should not be underestimated. However it is not completely impossible to link the two and organise a smooth and efficient appointment system that runs in tandem with the rest of the surgery.

The speed, intensity and volume of work is the most striking feature of counselling in the surgery, distinguishing it from counselling in other settings, and ultimately the open-door nature of primary care, where large numbers of patients stream through each week, is the fundamental influence on the work of the counsellor.

Summary

Counselling in primary care must be an integrated part of the whole. All team members need to develop strategies to achieve optimum integration. Where an atmosphere of intimacy is desirable, such as in the patient–counsellor relationship, careful attention should be paid to creating the appropriate ambiance. Equally, the way appointments are organised, external noise control and preventing interruptions are vital to the success of the encounter. Such a heightened awareness may be a new experience for some members of the team. Sensitivity to detail is not easily learned and can be a potential cause of friction for those team members who do not appreciate its value.

Counsellors must not underestimate their own need to adapt to their new situation as counsellors in primary care. They may have become accustomed to working with homogeneous clusters, and it may come as a surprise to them to discover a host of disparate presenting problems for which they may or may not have been prepared in advance. Their patients will come from a variety of social, ethnic, cultural, religious and economic backgrounds. But the excitement of counselling in primary care is precisely the variety and unpredictability of the work it brings. While there can be no better training than constantly responding to this shifting pageant of presenting patients, many counsellors find the lack of continuity and the uncertainty alarming to deal with. Flexibility is crucial and the counsellor is called on to apply creatively the techniques learned during training.

A broad base of skills is vital to the counsellor: astute assessment, compassionate counselling within a range of modalities with individuals, couples, families and groups in a time-limited, focused context. They also need to be familiar with different counselling orientations such as psychodynamics, cognitive and supportive therapy, and directive and non-directive approaches. If a patient needs complementary services that are not available in the surgery, the counsellor needs to be aware of the mechanisms for accessing appropriate resources. If all these skills are brought into play, counselling can come to resemble that long-forgotten breed of professional, the social caseworker. Although they have had their day, the caseworker once stood at the centre of their patients lives, helping to bridge the gap between the often confused inner world of feelings and fantasies and the outer world of practical realities, the function that we have now delegated to our counsellors.

4

REFERRALS: WHO REALLY NEEDS THE COUNSELLING?

Referrals in a primary care setting

Patients present with a wide range of emotional and psychological problems, often in the context of physical illness. Primary care is the most common place for people to seek professional help, and the onus is on GPs to listen to their patients and try to explore and understand more about what is troubling them. Ideally the GP will endeavour to make a diagnosis and management plan. He or she may choose to encourage the patient to return, may simply leave it vague, or may suggest a referral to another health professional either inside or outside the practice.

Referral can present a number of dilemmas. To whom are the patients to be referred: a psychiatrist, a social worker, a support group, a housing officer or a counsellor? In the latter case, is counselling appropriate for the patients, and are they sufficiently motivated to think about the meaning of their symptoms? What is the most appropriate referral procedure? In the case of an outside referral, are there NHS resources, and if so, will the waiting list be lengthy? Are there private counsellors or therapists in the area and do they have a good reputation? Are GPs ideologically comfortable with the idea of private referrals? Would some patients do better with a counsellor with one particular orientation rather than another? All these questions could understandably deter a busy GP from pursuing a referral for some form of counselling.

Finding an appropriate language with which to discuss referrals is essential. GPs and counsellors usually come from different training cultures, and because of this there may be real difficulties that must be negotiated before they can fully understand each other and achieve a workable cooperation in providing adequate patient care. Interprofessional problems of rivalry, envy and misunderstanding are bound to arise when professionals from different disciplines try to work together as a team. There may be mutual anxieties about competence, professional responsibility and inevitable struggles with appropriate boundaries of confidentiality. Doctors have relationships with their patients that extend over many years. They may feel reluctant to share their patients with other professionals for fear of spoiling the relationships they have built, or they may feel that they should be able to cope with all the problems themselves. They can be suspicious of the adequacy of a psychological approach for immediate, practical problems presented in the practice, or they may not know much about counselling or psychotherapy, its appropriateness, benefits and dangers (see Chapter 2 on the doctor–counsellor relationship).

Counsellors too come from a variety of training backgrounds and differ widely in both the amount and type of training they have had. They may neglect physical problems or organic illness, and in some cases have insufficient experience to understand the needs of the wider range of patients who present in primary care. Some have little experience of carrying out assessments and many become entrenched in a specific theoretical orientation that blinkers them to the particular needs of the context in which they are working. Many come into the surgery after working alone in private practice.

Implicit in any discussion about GP referrals is the notion of *trust*. Whether a referral is made to a specialist within or outside the practice, GPs are bound by GMC and BMA ethical guidelines to refer to those professionals whose competence is recognised by statutory regulations. Trust, which is not measurable in these terms, depends on a number of factors: an understanding of the professional's relevant skills and boundaries of competence, previous experience of good collaborative work and patient care, and some capacity for learning a common language so that communication can be fruitful.

The changing culture of referrals

The 1990s have brought huge changes to our mental health services. There has been a gradual closure of many of the hospitals housing large populations of mentally ill patients, and government policies have meant the transfer of mental health services from the traditional hospital setting out into the community. During the implementation of these changes there has been a fundamental reorganisation of services that were developed out of *need* to services determined by *market forces*, where the relationship between purchaser and provider is now the crucial factor. There has been a corresponding shift of power away from those providing mental health services towards those who are likely to purchase those services (Garelick and Wiener, 1996).

GPs are now heavily involved in the planning and provision of services in the community, which gives them considerable power. It is within the authority of practices, particularly if they are fundholding, to decide whether they wish to locate a counselling provision within the practice or to buy counselling, psychology or psychotherapy services from sources outside the practice, for example from private practitioners or from local NHS services, such as psychotherapy or psychology departments.

Menzies Lyth (1988) makes the point that public and government pressures can place incompatible demands on what she calls 'humane institutions', that is, those whose through-put material is human. A practice may be said to have custodial, therapeutic and financial objectives, and trying to meet one set of objectives may seriously inhibit achievement of the others. Recent media coverage suggests that stress is an increasing problem for doctors. Ever-increasing administrative pressures, lack of resources in the health and social services, the fear of complaints and a seemingly overwhelming need among patients can lead the stressed GP into a narrow, tunnel-vision view of the range of possible avenues available to help patients. The lethargy and repetitive behaviour that result from stress are likely to restrict the doctor's capacity to think imaginatively when discussing possible treatment options with patients. Consequently GPs may unconsciously avoid discussion of emotional issues and fail to diagnose depression and anxiety in their patients. Alternatively they may make hasty referrals to the counsellor or a hospital out-patient clinic to try to unload some of their patients and their problems. Working closely with a counsellor, sharing the stress, discussing patient assessments and possible management options can be one creative way of getting out of the tunnel into the light.

The impact of government changes

Since 1990, primary care has been subjected to a number of different pressures to modify its services, with significant effects on the referral culture. These pressures could be thought of as stemming from three different though overlapping sources. Garelick and Wiener (1996) subdivide the pressures into the *political*, the *social* and the *personal*.

Political pressures

- A shift of emphasis from clinical to financial criteria.
- General demands for audit and evaluation of work.
- Idealisation of the expected benefits of particular interventions.
- Pressure for a style of work where the outcome is easily measurable, both quantitatively and financially.
- Pressure to optimise budgets and maximise the number of patients seen.

Social pressures

- A shift towards mental health consumerism, where it is deemed desirable for individuals and communities to be consulted about the service provisions they require.
- Pressures arising from the move away from recognition of the value of a range of complementary approaches towards an atmosphere of competition, denigration and rivalry between them.
- Pressure to take on board a series of increasingly stringent demands from *outside* authorities, which limit and suppress the opportunities for individual creative thinking and new ideas.

Personal pressures

- Pressure caused by the clinical satisfaction of the job being eroded by ever-increasing political, financial and administrative demands.
- Personal conflict and stress resulting from what might be seen as perverse splits in the institutions of authority. On the one hand there is a demand to increase the services and training provision in primary care. On the other hand there is a diminishing pool of resources with which to achieve this.
- Radical change from job security and continuity to an atmosphere of uncertainty and insecurity about the future.
- Pressure to cut budgets and maximise the number of patients seen.
- Pressures that attack the value of specialist professional training and experience.

Whilst a few of these new pressures bring a welcome rigour to the evaluation of clinical work, including referrals for counselling, many are depressing and detract from the possibility of energetic attempts to expand and develop mutually rewarding teamwork opportunities.

Enhancing the GP's attitude towards counselling

The presence of an increasing number of counsellors in primary care suggests that some aspects of the referral culture have the potential to change. Göpfert and Barnes (1994) put forward the view that this will only be possible if GPs are able make a shift from the perception that problems are just located in the patient, towards the possibility that they may partly reside between GP and patient. They highlight the need for changes in the content of medical training practice to encourage doctors to develop more sophisticated relationships to psychological problems, and are optimistic that such changes will then allow doctors to use counsellors and psychotherapists differently: 'a counsellor in the practice could then become the carrier of an alternative *consultation culture* within primary care in psychologically-minded and non psychologically-minded practices alike' (quoted in East, 1995, p. 48).

It is generally understood that doctors find psychological problems in primary care the most challenging part of their clinical work. As described above, in a culture where GPs are under increasing pressure to take on more administrative work, interest and the mental space to focus on these problems may be diminishing, and in our experience the presence of a counsellor in the practice is likely to offer GPs relief in the form of a valuable additional resource and considerable emotional support. However some GPs have voiced doubts, saying that having a counsellor in the practice may have the effect of making them feel deskilled and nervous about trusting their own listening abilities and observational and counselling skills (see Chapter 1 on the hopes and realities of the work). It is interesting to note that the Royal College of General Practitioners has recently established a national programme of education in consultation skills so that doctors may improve their personal skills in diagnosing depression and anxiety, but in these times of change it is unlikely that GPs will be able to do all their own counselling.

Campkin advocates that further counselling training should take place in the practice, using the practice-based counsellor as a resource for the whole team:

with increasing involvement of all members of the primary care team in direct patient contact and care, they too could benefit by taking part in ways relevant to their own work. This is not in order to turn them all into counsellors, but to enable the 'counselling attitude' to prevail throughout the practice (Campkin, 1995, p. 263).

In our view the presence of a counsellor is more likely to facilitate improved GP counselling skills than to undermine them, and it is essential for doctors to have a good understanding of the counselling process if they are to make appropriate referrals to counsellors. GPs need to understand how patients may be helped to think about their difficulties, and in particular to know the kind of questions they should be asking in a range of different circumstances.

CASE EXAMPLE: MRS COURTNEY

Mrs Courtney is an intelligent, middle-class woman in her late fifties with a responsible job. She sees one of the female GPs in the practice fairly regularly for a minor medical problem and to talk about family worries. She is divorced from her husband, who is now dying from a long-term illness. Her son died a few years ago in slightly mysterious circumstances while at university. She visits the GP about once a month and this seems to be sufficient to contain her anxiety about her medical and emotional problems. This pattern begins to change and Mrs Courtney asks for more frequent appointments, telling the GP that she cannot cope. She becomes distressed and tearful every time she talks about her daughter. The GP asks what happened recently to make her feel so upset and she tells the GP that her daughter has become disturbed, sometimes suicidal, and has angry outbursts at her. She is worried that her daughter will kill herself, visits her every weekend, and is exhausted and at the end of her tether. The GP sensitively explores what Mrs Courtney is most worried about and realises that the imminent death of her estranged husband and the fragile state of mind of her daughter have aroused feelings that she must, at all costs, keep her daughter – the only surviving member of her nuclear family – alive. This, the GP realises, is an enormous burden. She helps Mrs Courtney to see that she needs more support, both for herself and in order to try to help her daughter, who will not accept professional help. Mrs Courtney is relieved to have 'been heard' and gratefully accepts a referral to the practice counsellor.

When to refer?

It is to the GP that patients often turn when they first make the important decision to talk about their problem, and GPs need to be alert to the emotional significance that this event is likely to have for their patients. A GP who prematurely says to him- or herself 'this is an emotional problem' and decides on an immediate referral to the counsellor, may leave the patient feeling frightened, mistrustful or rejected, and therefore uncontained. In our experience a GP will do well to see a patient several times in order to facilitate a consultation with another health professional within the practice. Immediate referrals, when the GP may not have allowed sufficient time to engage with the patient in order adequately to diagnose the problem, or when the GP is anxious that she or he may be about to open a Pandora's Box and 'dumps' the patient, may mean that the patient in question is less likely to make or keep an appointment with the counsellor.

CASE EXAMPLE: MR O'HARA

Mr O'Hara is in his sixties and has been with the practice for many years. His wife died three years ago and ever since he has been persecuted by feelings of guilt that he did not pay her enough attention or show her that he loved her. Last year he had an operation for bowel cancer. He tells the GP (who has looked after him through his bereavement and his illness) that he is still feeling very depressed. At the same time one of his children has been to see the GP, worried that his father has lost interest in life, spends every day at the pub and is drinking heavily. The GP immediately suggests a referral to the practice counsellor. Mr O'Hara dutifully attends the first appointment with the counsellor but is reluctant to talk about his troubles. The counsellor picks up his strong attachment to the GP when he talks of his gratefulness for the GP's patience in listening to his problems and for the excellent medical care he received throughout his illness. Mr O'Hara agrees when the counsellor suggests that he may feel more comfortable talking to the GP, and the session ends.

Later the counsellor meets with the GP in question and both agree that Mr O'Hara's depression has infected the GP, en- gendering a feeling of hopelessness about his skills in managing

risis. The GP had temporarily lost touch with the
f this patient's feelings of attachment to him and
l referral that the patient did not want, preferring
alk about his problems with the GP.

Who to refer?

les of counsellors in primary care settings has
cribed in the research literature. However
stigated the kinds of patient who tend to
ce counsellor. Two studies suggest that
varied and are likely to include family
s, instances of substance misuse and
.., 1988; Sibbald *et al.*, 1996). Research into
. of referrals is difficult because of the many
...ent kinds of counsellor currently employed in practices. Few
counsellors are likely to be skilled in a wide range of different
techniques and many choose to see those patients with whom they
feel most comfortable. GPs and counsellors should meet regularly to
decide which kinds of referral are appropriate and which are
inappropriate. In our experience the appropriateness of referrals is
likely to improve the longer the counsellor has been working in the
practice, and the more the counsellor and the GP are able to discuss
the referrals and to learn from their mistakes.

Sibbald *et al.* (1996) investigated the role of counsellors in primary
care, and found that 63 per cent of GPs participating in their study
referred patients with stress or anxiety problems to the counsellor;
42 per cent referred patients with relationship problems and 40 per
cent referred patients who were depressed. In addition, 26 per cent
of GPs referred patients suffering from bereavement and 26 per cent
referred those with a phobia or obsessional problems. Approximately 40 per cent of GPs would not refer patients who showed
evidence of psychotic illness.

Patients with the problems listed above are indeed likely to be
those who are most frequently referred, but if the GP and counsellor
have developed a relationship where discussion is possible and they
are able to do joint work, this is likely to facilitate the referral of a
wider range of patients. Elderly patients, patients with a psychiatric
history whose illness is under control, patients with psychosomatic
problems and patients from a variety of ethnic minority groups can
all do useful work with the counsellor.

Reasons for referral

GPs may decide to make a referral just because the counsellor has a vacancy, no more than that. In these days of financial pressure, it may be difficult for a GP to allow a counsellor any room for administration, supervision or merely time to think. Unused vacancies may be frowned upon. We have heard of GPs insisting that counsellors only see their patients for thirty or forty-five minutes, which suggests that GPs are trying to find ways of ensuring their counsellors are fully employed.

CASE EXAMPLE: REFERRAL PRACTICES

It has been an interesting exercise to compare GP referral patterns in our own different practices.

Practice 1

In the practice of one of the authors, the GPs employ three counsellors. One of the female GPs refers to the female counsellor patients who are bereaved and those who have small children, while patients with long-standing relationship problems and depression are referred to the second male counsellor. The third counsellor, also a man, receives the aggressive, psychotic or angry patients. In this case it is difficult to know the extent to which this behaviour is based on the GP's accurate perceptions of the counsellors' skills with particular patients, or whether it is based on less rational projections that are more to do with her own personality.

Practice 2

In the second practice the GPs employ a counsellor as well as a clinical psychologist, who is seconded to the practice by the local NHS psychology department for a session a week. Referrals in this practice seem to be made on a more straightforward basis. The clinical psychologist, who specialises in cognitive analytic therapy and cognitive behavioural therapy, is referred those patients who are likely to benefit from a more structured approach to dealing with stress and anxiety. The psychodynamic counsellor is referred those patients who are perceived to be psychologically minded and who, in the mind of the GP, will be more open to discovering the reasons behind their current problems and more capable of making psychological links.

Patients referred to the counsellor may be divided into new patients and those who are returning to see the counsellor after one or more previous visits. This latter situation is unique to primary care, and may be referred to as the 'revolving door syndrome', where the open system allows patients to visit their doctors or other specialists at any time. Some patients decide they do not want help after the assessment interviews, but may return some time later in a different frame of mind.

In general referrals to the practice counsellor are likely to be fairly informal. The referral may be for an assessment, for short-term treatment or in some cases for problem management. If the waiting list is not too long, it is possible to provide speedy intervention. In this setting there is much scope for *mixed therapies*, and it is not unusual for a counsellor to recommend to the GP that a patient be given medication between assessment sessions. In contrast referrals out of the practice to specialist clinics are inevitably more formal, involve a longer process and are usually for longer-term therapy.

What do GPs expect from a referral?

GPs tend to have three different expectations when making a referral to the counsellor. Sometimes these are conscious, at other times they are unconscious.

First, the GP may want further information about a patient. This may have a number of more or less obvious aims:

- At the simplest level the GP may wish to have a second opinion about the patient. This will provide psychological input into any treatment decisions made by the GP.
- On other occasions GPs may want something more than psychological input. They may actually want some insight into the patient's psychopathology, which can be used to make future treatment plans. The GP may also wish to learn more about the counsellor's way of working, which may contribute to the GP's own style of work with patients.
- There may be a less-conscious wish for the counsellor to help contain some of the anxiety generated in the GP by the particular patient.

A second expectation the GP may have from the referral is for the counsellor to take charge of the management of the case, which may include a referral out of the practice. Usually this is an expectation that the counsellor, if competent at assessment and knowledgeable about local (mental) health services, is well able to meet.

Finally, there is an area of expectation, often unconscious, that happens when a GP finds a particular patient unbearable or very difficult and wishes to dump or get rid of the patient. A referral to a counsellor in these circumstances may well cause problems later if the counsellor recommends joint management of the patient within the practice.

What do counsellors expect from the referral?

Most counsellors seek referrals that are appropriate to the counselling skills which they possess. It is not surprising that there is a wish to have 'nice' patients who are psychologically minded, motivated and able to communicate. However most patients in primary care do not meet these criteria and require much assessment skill. Expectations about the referral and the referral process vary widely among counsellors. Some wish to have information about a patient before the patient is seen and it is not uncommon for GPs to write referral letters to the counsellor. Others prefer to meet the patient 'fresh', to be informed by their own countertransference reactions without bias from the patient's notes or the GP's opinions.

After the assessment, expectations regarding further communication with the patient's GP again may vary. Many counsellors look for opportunities to feed back to the GP what they have learned about a patient and their treatment recommendations. Other counsellors, who wish to preserve the privacy of the patient–counsellor dyad, are likely to prefer to keep their evaluation to themselves (see Chapter 8 on key professional issues).

Problems in the referral process

Good counselling depends on the selection of good referrals. It is worth questioning why a GP refers a particular patient at a particular time. The question 'why now?' is a useful yardstick for GP and counsellor alike when thinking about why patients have presented themselves at one particular time rather than another. Of all the patients GPs see with emotional problems, why do they choose to work with some personally, refer some to the counsellor or other agency and ignore or do very little work with others? Some referrals are quite straightforward but we do not underestimate the number of unconscious forces at work that affect referral decisions. These are likely to operate in three main areas: the *power of the patient* to affect relationships between professionals; *unconscious factors* at work in the GP and counsellor; and the *atmosphere within the practice team* at the time of referral.

The power of the patient

Certain groups of patients are difficult to help and are likely to arouse feelings in the doctor that make the referral process difficult to manage:

- 'Difficult practice patients' have often been referred to a wide range of potential helpers, but always appear back in the practice to 'persecute' the doctor and often the receptionists too!
- Psychosomatic patients produce symptoms as a substitute for expressing feelings and can be difficult to help; counselling may exacerbate their illness.
- Patients with compulsive problems, for example eating disorders, may metaphorically 'throw up' offers of help as they may be more comfortable using food and/or laxatives to control their emotions.
- Teenagers with problems may not want to attend the practice, seeing doctors and therapists as parents or authority figures against whom they must rebel.
- Disturbed families can be difficult to work with because they rely on splitting within the family, usually selecting one member as 'the one with the problem'.
- Elderly people are often neglected, as there is a common belief that they are too set in their ways to be able to accept help and to change.
- Patients from some ethnic groups can be inaccessible to 'talking help' and counsellors may not understand their culture and language.
- Borderline and psychotic patients may be difficult to refer because their disturbance and anxiety can confuse and disorientate staff.

Tom Main (1989a) explained why some kinds of patient can be difficult. They convey great suffering but at the same time an insatiability, so that 'every attention is ultimately unsatisfying'. Behind this suffering, Main believes there is an in-built, primitive, psychological attack which demands that the helper takes on endless masochistic responsibility: 'you must go on helping me as so far, nothing you have done is making me better'.

Patients are bound to affect the doctor. If the doctor can reflect on this and think about what sometimes belongs to the patient and what is part of the doctor's own emotional make-up, the assessment and referral of the patient can be improved by intuitively understanding the painful feelings of the patient, assimilating them, and then sympathetically describing them to the patient. Often the power of the patient may be such that the doctor's capacity to think and reflect is impaired, leading to the substitution of action for thought and a hasty referral, as illustrated by the case of Mr O'Hara above.

Unconscious factors in the GP and counsellor that affect referrals

One of the strongest pressures on GPs is to 'do something', to take some action that will make the patient better quickly. To achieve a cure is one of the main objectives of the medical approach, and as Tom Main says: 'cured patients do great service to their attendants' (Main, 1989a p. 12). The treatment of psychological problems is not so much about cure as about trying to help people understand themselves better so that they can manage their lives more effectively. A psychodynamic approach places great value on subjective rather than objective knowing, so that the doctor's personal response to the patient may be used as a helpful tool for diagnosis, referral and treatment. For instance if the GP feels depressed by a patient, it is likely that the patient is depressed too. Similarly if the GP feels angry, the patient may well be feeling, but not expressing, anger. However using our own 'antennae' can be tricky because, as we have outlined, some patients overwhelm us with their feelings, while others are inaccessible.

Patients can stir up the GP or counsellor in a number of different ways, affecting referral decisions. There are three different responses:

- *The omnipotent approach*: rushing around trying to do everything. This may foster overdependent relationships and encourage patients to project too much power into the doctor and not take sufficient responsibility for their own difficulties.

- *The defensive approach*: switching off from the patient's distress. Reaching for the prescription pad is one way of avoiding emotional problems. Overconcentrating on physical symptoms, investigations and specialist referrals is another. We could view the ten-minute consultation as a device to avoid really getting to know our patients.
- *The anxious approach*: where patients' anxiety may overwhelm GPs and propel them into action rather than reflection.

We have found that the following groups of patients have particularly powerful emotional effects, sometimes making the GP or counsellor behave uncharacteristically:

- Psychosomatic patients can generate anxiety about the possibility of missing real physical disease.
- Patients who present problems of great urgency can be overwhelming and create intense pressure to do something immediately.
- Seriously depressed patients can project their depression, paralysing the professionals and engendering feelings of hopelessness and despair.
- Self-destructive patients, including patients with addictions, can be very disturbing and intolerable.
- Professionals enjoy a certain amount of dependency on the part of patients because it makes them feel needed, but they may well feel anxious and uneasy when dealing with highly dependent and vulnerable patients.
- Sometimes the patient's problem is too close to home. For instance a recent bereavement may make it difficult for the GP or counsellor to work effectively with bereaved patients.
- Patients who are out of touch with their feelings can leave the professionals feeling helpless and out of touch too.
- Professionals may 'act out' in response to a very likeable patient, with too much attention or concern, which may not always be in the patient's best interest.
- Finally there are those patients who, for one reason or another, the doctor or counsellor simply does not like or want to help.

If GPs are able to share their thoughts and feelings about a patient, this will help the counsellor to understand why that particular patient is being referred. Together they can then think about the potential doctor–patient–counsellor relationship. It may become clear that the referral has more to do with how the doctor feels than what the patient wants or needs. Sometimes counsellors can help GPs deal with the feelings the patient is projecting onto them, enabling useful work to continue with the patient without a referral. At other times the counsellor may agree to see a patient for a while, until the doctor is able to tolerate and work with the patient again

Referrals to the counsellor can be inappropriate and the patient may fail to turn up. We have found that a good number of these patients have been 'pushed' by the doctor into seeing the counsellor because the doctor was finding it difficult to work with the patient for one of the reasons listed above. Unless this is understood, the counsellor may well feel that he or she has been 'dumped' with impossible patients, leading to feelings of resentment. On the other hand, if feelings about difficult patients can be acknowledged they are more likely to be used constructively to make realistic and appropriate management plans, to deepen the doctor–counsellor relationship and to manage more patients effectively on a long-term basis within the practice.

The following example illustrates what can happen when GPs are unable to separate their own difficulties from those of their patients, leading to a series of 'inappropriate' referrals.

CASE EXAMPLE: DR HILL

A female doctor refers to the counsellor a series of women with what the doctor calls 'eating problems'. Many of these women are slightly overweight. Most of them are not motivated to seek help, in fact, they do not see themselves as having a problem with eating or their weight. They feel that they are only responding to the doctor's opinion that they ought to see the counsellor. It takes some time to realise that the doctor is herself getting thinner and thinner, verging on anorexia! In this case the issue is not addressed directly between the counsellor and GP as the counsellor has been in the practice for only a short time and is still somewhat in awe of the GP's status. It seems too much of an intrusion into the GP's privacy. However, having realised what is happening, the counsellor is able to let the patients leave without worrying about them too much.

Practice dynamics and their effect on referrals

In some cases patients and their particular problems mirror some of the current problems in the practice as a whole. Referrals are affected by the atmosphere in the practice team, and the following examples illustrate how patients may become symptoms of practice dynamics.

CASE EXAMPLE: DR MILLER

One of the female partners, who has been in the practice for about six months, begins to refer a number of middle-aged, depressed women who are struggling to make a life for themselves after their children have left home. In many cases their husbands are emotionally unavailable. The counsellor begins to realise that some of these women do not want to see her, but have been sent by the GP. The counsellor has a good relationship with this GP and it is possible to talk about what is going on. What emerges is that the GP was left with a large number of older, middle-class women when another female partner left the practice. When asked why she is making all these referrals, the new doctor realises that she is experiencing difficulty with these women because they remind her of her own mother, who has recently been widowed. The referrals reflect some of the difficulties experienced by the practice in adjusting to changes in the partnership, as well as some of the GP's personal and private struggles.

CASE EXAMPLE: FINANCIAL PROBLEMS

A second incident arose at a time when there was intense conflict in the practice, making it extremely difficult for the GPs to work together and leading eventually to a decision by the GPs concerned to split up. Some of this conflict centred on arguments about money and the deployment of practice resources. Within a two-month period, two patients were referred to the counsellor for assessment: one was in danger of being declared bankrupt; the other was involved in shady, possibly fraudulent dealings. Unconsciously the GPs were expressing some of their own anxieties in the referrals, and were hoping that the counsellor could help them with their own dilemmas.

Menzies Lyth (1988) believes that primitive anxieties are always present in all organisations and social structures. Influenced by the writings of Klein and Bion, she explores how the very structure of an institution can be seen as a form of defence, designed to avoid or minimise personal experiences of doubt, guilt, anxiety and uncertainty. At times this defensive structure is actually antisupportive to staff:

> the need of the members of the organisation . . . to use it in the struggle against anxiety . . . leads to the development of socially structured defence mechanisms as elements in the organisation's structure, culture and mode of functioning (Menzies Lyth, 1988, p. 50).

'Busyness' in primary care is a good example of a defence against uncertainty and anxiety. In each of the above examples, where events in the practice and the particular difficulties faced by each doctor are affecting referrals, time can be wasted in the pursuit of a course of action that leads into a cul-de-sac. A GP may not consciously make the link between what is going on in the practice and the way patients are being dealt with; the patients do not understand why they are being referred, and the counsellor may wonder what on earth is going on. Clearly it is helpful if the counsellor is sufficiently immersed in the practice dynamics to understand some of the issues involved. Creating structures to review referrals, where there is time to reflect and talk about them, is the most effective way of minimising unconscious actions that are likely to be unhelpful to patients.

Qualitative research into referral patterns

After two years of working in a practice, one of the authors and a GP partner decided to study referrals to the practice counsellor, why the patients had been referred and what had happened to them after their assessment (Dammers and Wiener, 1995). The study looked at referrals over a four-year period. In the first two years the four GPs in the practice made 101 referrals to the counsellor, who was employed for four hours a week in a practice with approximately 6000 patients. (The limited number of hours this counsellor worked in the practice restricted her role to assessment and some short-term work, although she saw a few patients intermittently over a longer term.) Two years later the exercise was repeated to see if patterns had changed. What happened to patients after referral was examined after the first two years, and again two years later, and are presented for comparison in Table 4.1.

Table 4.1 Referrals from GPs to a counsellor in one practice: comparison between patients referred in two one-year periods

	1988/9	*1990/1*
Assessment and referral for long-term work – taken up	28	14
Assessment and referral for long-term work – not taken up	14	3
Assessment followed by short-term work in the practice	12	25
Assessment followed by joint management with GP in the practice	14	20
Assessment only – patient expressed no wish for further help	14	16
Patient left in the middle of the initial assessment	11	11
Patient failed to attend the initial assessment	8	12
Total number of patients seen in each 2-year period	101	101

The most significant change over the four-year period was that the longer the counsellor had been employed in the practice, the fewer patients were referred outside the practice for long-term work. In addition, the counsellor took longer to make her initial assessments and also took on a larger proportion of patients for short-term work. She became more flexible in her approach to treatment and a greater number of difficult patients were taken on for active joint management with the GP. The GPs also became more confident in their ability to assess and manage patients themselves, and more open to talking about some of their patients with the counsellor, without actually referring them. The number of patients for whom an assessment only was sufficient, remained constant. It is interesting to note that the number of patients who failed to attend their assessment appointment also remained constant, although it was expected that as the relationship between counsellor and GP deepened, and the counsellor developed more skills working in primary care, the number of missed appointments would decrease.

Summary

The research described above demonstrates how, over time, the quality of referrals improves when the GPs and counsellors involved begin to learn a common language, a finding that is surely generalisable to all practices. If GPs develop a more realistic understanding of what counsellors can and cannot do, and counsellors come to understand the milieu of primary care and to appreciate more fully the nature of GPs' work, particularly with patients with long-term relationships with the practice, then joint work will become rewarding for both. Time must be made to review the work, to discuss problems, to try to learn from mistakes and to understand each other's strengths and weaknesses. Relationships with counsellors as members of the practice team will then become more highly valued, not only by the doctors, but also by the paramedical staff and receptionists, and inevitably the quality of referrals, their timing and appropriateness will improve.

5

ASSESSMENT FOR COUNSELLING AND TREATMENT OPTIONS

Introduction

Both authors enjoy doing assessments. We are not sure whether or not we could postulate an archetype (Jung, 1934) of curiosity as ubiquitous for all psychotherapists, but in the course of our work the *frisson* of anticipation is often heightened when seeing someone for an initial consultation. Patients' anxiety about revealing their story to a stranger, often for the first time in their lives, cannot but infuse the atmosphere in the room with a special tension.

Surveying some of the literature on assessment, we have been struck by the quality of alert excitement that authors use to describe their personal responses to the assessment situation, which is suggestive of 'a first date'. Holmes (1995, p. 27) compares his feelings before an assessment to the start of a theatrical performance: 'slight tension, pleasurable anticipation, anxiety about how I and the patient are going to perform'. Coltart (1993, p. 59) likens it to reading a novel: 'I will be the privileged possessor of an entirely new story. It is as good as starting a new novel'.

Assessments are likely to form a large part of the clinical work for counsellors working in primary care. One paradox in our culture is that many more people are now seeking counselling, but in an atmosphere of public scepticism about and attack upon its benefits. The increasing number of different types of counselling and therapy from which to choose means that careful assessment is even more relevant now than in the past, and the expectations of potential patients about what they may gain from counselling or psychotherapy are likely to increase. Moreover, the aetiological understanding of psychopathology has developed enormously over the past fifty years with increasing knowledge about the effect of the early stages of life on later human development. Two registration bodies for psychotherapy, the United Kingdom Council for Psychotherapy (UKCP) and the British Confederation of Psychotherapists (BCP) have been formed to protect the interests of the public and to exercise control over training standards and ethical clinical practice. The UKCP encompasses organisations practising a broad range of psychotherapies while the BCP is made up of organisations with a psychodynamic orientation.

In our view the assessment situation is inevitably tense because two sometimes incompatible aims must be pursued simultaneously within a short space of time. The assessor must try to create a safe enough atmosphere for sufficient unconscious material to emerge so that he or she may glean something of the internal world of the patient–a more reflective mode of being–while at the same time gathering relevant factual information–a more active mode of being. Although the literature is growing, at the time of writing, there are, relatively few papers on assessment and these are confusing since the authors are writing about assessment for different things, for example counselling, analysis, patients' suitability for inexperienced trainees. We have found ourselves wondering whether assessment, with its emphasis on history taking, psychodynamic formulation and diagnosis, is perhaps dissonant with the fundamental aims of counselling. Discussions of psychopathology and symptoms that emphasise the need to place a patient firmly in a diagnostic category do not necessarily sit comfortably with the mysteries of individuation, which emphasise the unique nature of each individual and the possibility that symptoms can be creative.

The metaphor of Janus

The metaphor of Janus is helpful when thinking about assessment. Janus was the Roman god of beginnings who kept the gate of heaven and became the guardian of gates and doors. He is often portrayed as having two faces looking in different directions. His insignias were a key, which opened and closed the door, and a *stick*, which porters employed to drive away those who had no right to cross the threshold. His two faces allowed him to observe both the exterior and the interior of the house and the entrance and exit of public buildings. Like Janus the assessor must always look in two different 'directions', so that he or she may hold both the intellectual and the affective in some kind of dialectic during the assessment interview. To develop this metaphor further, the nature of the environment in which the assessment is carried out means that assessors must retain their capacity for vigilance on both the vertical and the horizontal axis. They require an internal sentry to guard against invasions from their unconscious arising from the influences of the setting (vertical), and an actual sentry who tries to find ways of gauging the outside pressures on the assessment process (horizontal).

The aims of the assessment

Today the term *diagnosis*, with its psychiatric overtones, is rarely used. Counsellors are more inclined to talk of an *assessment*, a *consultation* or even an *initial interview*, and the search for a *psychodynamic formulation* is more relevant. The word assessment is generally used in the National Health Service and the Shorter Oxford English Dictionary defines an assessor as 'one who sits beside another or a person who shares another's position'. The term *consultation* is more usual in private practice and is defined as 'a meeting in which parties consult together, or one person consults another'. Whichever term is used, both definitions highlight the contrast between the more objective and distanced assessment of one person by another expert, and the greater mutuality of a meeting between two people where both will play a significant part in the outcome.

The literature on assessment also reflects these divisions. Some authors place more emphasis on the medical approach, listing the characteristics of analysability (Malan, 1979; Edwards, 1983; Kernberg, 1984; Coltart, 1993). Others place more emphasis on the quality and atmosphere of the first meeting and the interpersonal dynamics during the assessment process (Steiner, 1993; Hobson, 1985; Hinshelwood, 1995). Tensions between opposites, between the *art* and the *science* of assessment, between *knowing* and *not knowing*, between *empathy* and *distance*, between the *objective* and the *subjective* are of the essence at the time of an assessment interview, and these are familiar to us all as counsellors in the continuing struggle for relationship. Samuels (1989) calls these splits the 'professional' and the 'poetic' analytic attitude to assessment. Another way of putting it could be to say that the assessor must struggle to integrate the poetic with the professional through the smooth functioning of what Jung (1934) has called the 'transcendent function'; that psychological function which mediates opposites and facilitates a transition from one psychological attitude or state of mind to another.

The assessment process in primary care has six main aims:

- To find a way of engaging with the patient that will hopefully lead to a conversation where feelings may emerge and access to unconscious material becomes possible.
- At the end of our meeting(s), to emerge with a picture of the patient's relationships based on his or her life at present, in the past and through the relationship with the counsellor.
- To facilitate an open discussion with the patient about how to proceed and what kind of treatment plan will be most appropriate.
- To attend to and integrate the past and present relationship of the patient with the referring GP.
- To pay attention to and integrate the dynamics of the relationship between the assessor and the referring GP.
- To take account of any previous referrals to health professionals or specialists inside or outside the practice.

One of the advantages of a psychodynamic approach is that counsellors become skilled in using as an important subjective tool their own feelings and bodily responses to the patient. In psychodynamic language, this is about using the dynamics of transference/countertransference to make sense of the here and now relationship between assessor and patient. We have noticed that with experience assessors come to rely more heavily on their intuition and countertransference affects in the assessment situation. Often we form an impression of the patient within the first five minutes and spend the remaining time testing our hypothesis. This subtle balance between intuition/hunch and the capacity to sustain a space for clear thinking is of the essence in the assessment situation.

Assessment in a primary care setting

Many counsellors working in surgeries are employed for a limited number of hours, often between three and six hours a week. Because of this the main emphasis of the job is likely to be on assessment rather than on the actual treatment of patients. Whilst most counsellors are likely to have attended at least some seminars on assessment during the course of their training, many will arrive in the surgery with limited experience of assessing the wide range of patients with whom they will be presented. The reader will already have observed that both authors are of the opinion that assessment in primary care presents the counsellor with a very particular set of dynamics to manage. With the exception of Berkowitz (1996), as yet, there is little published literature on the vicissitudes of the assessment process in this environment.

The setting of the assessment interview has a significant influence on the process, and while assessors may bring their personal style and approach to the process, the environment constellates particular personal and collective unconscious forces within the assessor that can subtly affect the dynamics of the meeting with the patient and the quality of the assessment. Consider the following two quotations: 'assessment should be seen as an entity in its own right, with its own clinical technique' (Garelick, 1994, p. 101) 'there is no difference between the analytic process in the first meeting and that in any other meeting. The analyst in the initial meeting is no more or less an analyst, the analysand is no more or less an analysand, the analysis is no more or less an analysis than in any other meeting' (Ogden, 1989, p. 170). Here are two authors whose statements about their beliefs about assessment contradict each other. The differences between them can be explained if we attend to the context, roles and environment in which their ideas have emerged: Garelick is writing about assessments for psychotherapy in an NHS psychotherapy clinic; Ogden about the initial interview before himself taking a patient into analysis.

For the counsellor who works in the practice and comes from a training background where firm boundaries and structures are advocated, adjusting to work in this particular setting can be difficult. The counsellor is working on the premises and may need to be vigilant to forces from several different directions that may impinge on the assessment process. He or she, like Janus, may need to wield both the key and the stick at different times. There may be strong conscious or unconscious pressure to adopt a work-style like that of the GPs, with a fast through-put of patients seen for short periods of time, and to take on 'impossible patients'. The counsellor may have to struggle to achieve a delicate balance between flexibility in terms of work style and firm boundaries in order to ensure continuing space for the assessment process to evolve.

CASE EXAMPLE: DR FIELDING

A GP refers a woman to the practice counsellor for assessment. The GP says that he wonders if she might benefit from some counselling. The patient turns out to be a totally unsuitable referral. She is unapproachable, angry and at times psychotic and shouts at the counsellor throughout the session. The counsellor is puzzled by this referral from the doctor, who seems to be behaving out of character as he usually refers suitable patients with some motivation to understand their own difficulties. The counsellor knows this particular GP quite well and is able to discuss the referral with him. It emerges that the patient had been asked to leave a number of previous practices in the area as GPs found her to be endlessly demanding and often aggressive, and eventually – when nothing they did seemed to make any difference, and they could bear her no longer – she was pushed out. Unconsciously the GP needs the counsellor to know what a difficult time he is having and the referral is an expression of his own stressful workload. On realising this, she discusses with him the possibility of her supporting some of the difficult practice patients for a time as a way of relieving the overburdened GP.

Who is assessed?

Berkowitz (1996) highlights the duality of the assessment situation. She puts forward the idea that in general assessors should have two questions in the mind when they meet a new patient. First, 'Why now?' Why is this patient coming to see the counsellor at this particular point in time? Second, 'What is the way forward for this particular patient?' By now the reader will have gathered that both authors are of the opinion that the question of who is assessed in primary care involves not only the patient, but also, and most importantly, the working situation. Because counsellors are working on the practice premises as part of the practice team, the organisational dynamics of the practice inevitably affect the choice of patient a GP decides to refer to the counsellor (see Chapter 4 on referrals and Chapter 9 on research).

It is possible to divide the patients referred into those where the GP is behaving appropriately and consciously, and those where unconscious or neurotic factors, as in the case example above, are likely to mean that the patient is carrying a projection, feeling or state of mind on behalf of the GP.

Appropriate referrals

Many GPs, particularly those who are accustomed to working with a counsellor in the practice, become skilled at making sensitive judgements about which patients to refer to the counsellor for assessment, how to make a referral and at what point to encourage the patient to make an appointment with the counsellor. In general the GP may have a number of different thoughts going on in his or her mind when contemplating a referral:

- This patient is asking to see a counsellor.
- If I handle it carefully, this patient could benefit from seeing the counsellor.
- I am not sure whether to send this patient to a psychiatrist or to the counsellor. I will ask the counsellor for a second opinion.
- I have not got the time/skill to explore this patient's problems, I shall refer him/her to the counsellor instead.

Schachter (1990) lists the following patients as suitable for a referral to the practice counsellor:

- Those with psychological symptoms such as general anxiety, depression, repetitive relationship problems, grief reactions or ambivalence about a termination of pregnancy.
- Those with psychological problems who do not wish to be referred to health professionals outside the practice.
- Those who have problems related to life-stage transitions such as marriage, having children, leaving home, mid-life, aging, physical or terminal illness.
- 'Difficult practice patients', where a multidisciplinary or even a multi-agency approach is needed to 'hold' the patient.
- Some patients with chronic problems, either psychosocial or physical, where it is important to distinguish between those patients with chronic physical symptoms that may or may not be psychogenic in origin and those who suffer from well-recognised psychosomatic illnesses.
- Some patients with acute drug or alcohol problems.

The striking feature of this list is the wide range of problems a counsellor working in primary care may be asked to assess. This is in contrast to the assessment situation in an NHS psychotherapy department or in private practice, where patients have usually passed through a formal filtering process before they reach the psychotherapist. We would like to add two other categories of patient to Schachter's list:

- Elderly patients, many of whom can reap huge rewards from spending time with the counsellor in the practice.
- Those patients who have suffered recent trauma, for example rape or sudden accidents such as a car crash (Berkowitz, 1996).

Inappropriate referrals

GPs are often gripped by unconscious forces when deciding when and which patients should be referred to the counsellor. Patients who are 'special 'are often referred. These may be patients who are especially 'loved', but it is more likely that they are patients whom the GP finds difficult to deal with or may actively dislike. A common situation is the 'urgent referral', where particular patients are likely to arouse tension, anxiety or concern in the GP, which may result in a strong drive to take speedy action. Whilst on occasion speedy action may indeed be helpful, on many occasions the nature of the transference/countertransference dynamics between patient and GP can prevent GPs from thinking clearly about the effect their patients are having on them and why they feel pressure to act rather than reflect. On most occasions, when a GP asks the counsellor to fit in an urgent referral the assessment does not progress smoothly. Sometimes the patient simply does not turn up, on other occasions a particular dynamic operating between patient and GP becomes similarly constellated between patient and counsellor.

CASE EXAMPLE: MRS CHANDLER

A patient's wife comes to see one of the female GPs in the practice. Her husband had an accident the previous year and sustained a nasty blow to his head. Since then he has been drinking heavily and she is worried about his violent temper and his aggressive behaviour towards her and their children. She is very upset and asks the GP to encourage her husband to see the practice counsellor. The GP is worried about the family situation and asks the counsellor to fit him in as 'an urgent assessment'. Not surprisingly the husband fails to keep the appointment. Some time later, when the GP has herself seen the husband after an emergency weekend telephone call from the wife, it emerges that his drinking problem is serious and that he will require medical treatment before a referral to the counsellor can be of any use.

This GP was taken over and impelled to act by the man's wife rather than taking time to reflect about the family. It would undoubtedly have been better for the GP to have tried to see the husband first, before requesting what was a premature referral to the counsellor when direct medical intervention was more appropriate.

Making the assessment

Who is the assessment for?

In general a counsellor needs to hold in mind several different sets of needs when beginning the assessment:

- The needs of the GP, who holds overall responsibility for the patient's care.
- The fact that the assessment is for the patient, in order to discover what would be most helpful for him or her in terms of future treatment plans.
- Both political and audit factors when deciding what to recommend to the patient. Counselling in primary care takes place in a political context, where the emphasis is on seeing a large number of patients in as short a time as possible. Audit may also play a part, particularly with government recommendations for detailed records about numbers and types of patients seen, ethnic minority groups treated, frequency of sessions and so on.

The assessment process

A number of papers have been written on the areas to be covered in an assessment interview. As mentioned earlier in this chapter, one problem that is evident from reading these papers is that the authors are making assessments in different environments and with different sets of objectives. Some papers have been written on the assessment of suitable patients for private psychotherapy or analysis (Edwards; 1983; Limentani, 1989; Ogden, 1989; Coltart 1993; Steiner, 1993). Others write specifically about assessment for psychotherapy within NHS psychotherapy clinics (Garelick, 1994; Hinshelwood, 1995; Holmes, 1995). Little has been written about the specifics of the assessment interview in primary care.

We will outline what we do in practice, whilst recognising that there are no 'right' or 'wrong' strategies for carrying out an assessment. We acknowledge both similarities and differences in our personal ways of dealing with the assessment situation. The following is a list of key questions that are helpful to keep in mind during the course of an initial assessment interview in the surgery:

- Why is the patient here at this particular time?
- What was going on in the GP's mind to suggest a referral at this point in time?
- How does the patient feel about being here?
- What effect is this patient having on me?
- What is the nature of this patient's defences and how rigid are they?
- Are there particular internal or external events that originated in the patient's childhood and may be contributing to his or her current problem?
- How psychologically minded is this patient?
- Does this patient have sufficient ego strength to cope with counselling?
- Do I have the necessary skills to work with this patient?
- Do I have the time and resources to work with this patient in the practice or will he or she need to be referred outside the practice?
- Can I make a useful psychodynamic formulation about the patient and his or her difficulties?

Assessment and treatment

Assessment is the process of determining the nature of the patient's condition and what to do about it. Treatment, where indicated, can only begin once the assessment process has been completed. The search for information is more important during assessment and decision making will be an aim. Treatment moves at a completely different pace and has a different aim, yet it is not uncommon for counsellors to ignore the distinction between assessment and treatment. Some counsellors hold the view that treatment starts from the moment the patient enters the room – or even earlier – if transference can be said to begin before the patient reaches the counsellor's door, but if counsellors overlook the distinction between assessment and treatment, then patients are likely to ignore it too, and by default slip unwittingly into treatment the moment they walk into the room. It is therefore, vital, to seize a convenient moment to spell out to the patient the aims of the first meeting, its purpose, length and potential outcome. After the first assessment meeting is over the counsellor will have a number of options. The patient may be:

- Offered another interview to complete her or his assessment.
- Referred back to the GP, with no further contact anticipated.
- Offered further appointments for short- medium- or longer-term counselling.
- Offered a combination of psychotropic and counselling treatment.
- Referred elsewhere if more specialised treatment, unavailable in the surgery, is considered necessary, such as intensive individual, family, marital or group psychotherapy; or referred to a social club or social services.

CASE EXAMPLE: ANNE

At her first appointment Anne, a 35 year old woman, glares at the counsellor defiantly and refuses to talk. She says angrily that she doesn't want to see him. It was Dr H's idea. If he wants to find out what is wrong with her, he had better ask her questions. 'I am not the sort who gushes out to strangers', she growls. There follow periods of sullen silence, punctuated by remarks such as 'it's all a waste of time' and, 'nothing will ever change'. At times she is near to tears. The counsellor tries to help her express what she is feeling by acknowledging that it is difficult to talk to someone she does not know and may not see again. It is only towards the end of the appointment that she is able to reveal that her problem is an inability to form relationships with others.

Although she continues to dismiss the usefulness of the session right through to the end, the counsellor's efforts seem to put her at ease and he has the impression that she is hoping she will not be rejected. He has no factual information about her or her predicament, but her reactions to the session and his experience of her point to a hurt and vulnerable woman, frightened and untrusting. During the session she crudely reenacts the features of her previous failed relationships.

The counsellor tells Anne that as they have hardly begun to talk about the sources of her unhappiness, he hopes to see her again. She says that she does not want to come back, but if he particularly wants to see her she will keep the appointment.

At Anne's second appointment, four weeks later, she is calm, smiling, cooperative and willing to talk. In between appointments she has realised that it is pointless to be so defiant, something of a theme in her life. For the past ten years she has experienced a profound sense of meaninglessness. She has not been able to value herself, or anything she does. Pleasure has been absent from her life, leaving only endless boring routines.

An uneventful but reasonably happy childhood became a restless and unsettled adolescence and she was determined to 'break out'. She travelled overseas for six years and had a child, with whom she returned to England. After that her life revolved entirely around her work and mothering her child, both of which she did efficiently and lovingly, while a deep unhappiness persisted. She dwelt constantly on 'what if' scenarios and sensed that her life was increasingly restricted. Consequently she could not allow herself to have any wishes in case (1) they could not be fulfilled, and (2) she might 'break out' again and cause her daughter to suffer. The alternative was to wipe out all thoughts of self-fulfillment, but in the process she turned herself into a mindless jobber and grew angry and depressed.

At Anne's third session she works on some of the issues raised in the second, in particular the efficient, happy and independent worker/mother persona, and the frustrated, resentful, guilty and frightened woman underneath. She says she needs help but had been frightened of that too because she had heard that psychotherapy causes dependency. She talks about her ambivalent feelings and she is later successfully referred for long-term individual psychoanalytic psychotherapy.

To have offered Anne a predetermined number of sessions without first addressing her very angry feelings would have been pointless. She almost walked out of her first session! Here flexibility was the key, since it allowed Anne sufficient time to express her despair and hopelessness at ever being able to escape her trapped situation. Clearly this was a case where it was impossible to predict in advance what best to offer the patient. Was she suicidal? Would she return for her second session? A child was involved. There were risks, but the counsellor had to contain his anxiety and trust that sufficient emotional contact had been made with the patient to bring her back.

Another difficulty could have occurred at the point of the referral for psychotherapy, where fear of rejection and abandonment might have surfaced again and upset the plan. Anne had made an enormous leap of faith to place her trust in the counsellor, and at the end of three sessions she would have to take her leave and establish contact all over again with another stranger. Her previous experiences of loss stood to undermine the referral process. In suggesting that a patient be referred for individual psychotherapy outside the practice, the counsellor takes a calculated risk. The patient's need for help is recognised, but poor timing or an indiscreet remark about the seriousness of the problem could scupper the referral. Unless Anne's feelings of abandonment were adequately addressed at the close of counselling in the practice, her new counsellor could have become the target of these unresolved feelings, making for a difficult start to her therapy.

The above example highlights the importance of maintaining a distinction between the assessment process and treatment. Seeing patients in primary care allows for an extended assessment process and there is no need to complete the assessment in one session (Garelick, 1994). In an extended assessment, where the patient is seen several times, the counsellor has time and space to get to know the patient and decide with the patient the optimum treatment options. While it is of course true that the assessment situation inevitably has a treatment component (ibid.), inadequate training and an ignorance of institutional dynamics can make it extremely difficult for counsellors to maintain this essential distinction.

Frequency of assessment interviews

Counselling practice may vary here. One author of the present authors, for example, sees a patient for one session and it is only at the end of that session that he decides whether to see the patient again. The other author, when meeting the patient for the first time, usually suggests that it may be helpful to meet a number of times, in order to explore the nature of the patient's difficulties, before making any decisions about how to proceed. For many patients, meeting two or three times as part of the assessment is sufficient. For some there is an inevitable treatment component, even if it is not made explicit. On other occasions the counsellor may not have sufficient time to enter into an extended assessment or indeed may believe that the transference attachment of the patient to the counsellor is likely to become too intense if the assessment process is extended.

Spacing of assessment interviews

One of the benefits of working in a GP surgery is that many of the patients have been attached to the practice for a long time and have adapted to the natural rhythm of the practice as a whole, for example 'come and see me again in two weeks'. They can return to their GP for different reasons at different times. This has benefits for the busy counsellor with a waiting list, because if patients have to wait a few weeks until they are seen, the fact that the surgery is a familiar place is likely to be containing and can help the patient to bear the wait. Similarly if patients decide to end the assessment prematurely, it is usually possible for them to return at some future date when they are less resistant or anxious, or they may choose to talk about their assessment experiences with the GP.

Missed sessions

In general the non-attendance rate in primary care is high. It is not uncommon to hear of at least one patient in three failing to turn up. The reasons for this are varied. On some occasions the GP has been precipitate and forced a referral too early, without taking sufficient account of the patient's attachment. On other occasions the urgency of the situation diminishes. Sometimes it is the GP who wishes the patient to see the counsellor rather than the patient him or herself. At other times the patient is frightened and cancels the appointment, although, as mentioned above, some return at a later date.

Communication with the GP

An important theme highlighted throughout this book is both authors' commitment to a model of work that promotes the development of a common language between counsellor and GP. Appropriate boundaries of confidentiality are crucial, but should be held within the boundaries of the practice as a whole rather than tightly between counsellor and patient. With this in mind, it is essential that GPs should be informed about the outcome of counsellors' assessments of patients in the practice (see Chapter 8 on key professional issues).

Recommendations for treatment

A counsellor needs to take account of a number of different factors when trying to decide with the patient which treatment to pursue. Broadly these are likely to include what the patient and the counsellor feel will be most helpful for the patient, the resources inside and outside the practice and the views of the referring GP. In connection with what is *helpful for the patient*, the following will be relevant:

- The ego strength of the patient.
- The nature of the patient's defences.
- The patient's motivation.
- The patient's current support network, including friends, family, employment.
- The patient's history of acting-out, including breakdown, suicide attempts, drug and alcohol abuse.
- Whether the patient is motivated for counselling.

Second, the *resources in the practice* are likely to have a significant influence on any decisions made:

- The counsellor's availability to do short-term or extended work within the practice.
- The possibility of joint work/shared management with the GP or another member of the practice team.
- The skills and specialisms of the counsellor.
- The limits of the counsellor's skills. For example, a counsellor trained in individual work may not be competent or confident to undertake marital or family work.
- The availability of appropriate services outside the practice. These may include psychiatric services, NHS psychotherapy services, day hospitals and specialist counselling facilities including cancer counselling, HIV counselling, group, family or marital psychotherapy, counselling services for ethnic minority groups and so on.

Third, it is essential for the counsellor to take into account the *views and feelings of the GP* who referred the patient. If counsellors and GPs are to work successfully together, drawing up a joint treatment plan that takes account of the views of the patient, the counsellor and the GP is likely to feel more supportive and containing for the patient in the long run. With this in mind the following factors are likely to require consideration:

- The agreement of the GP to the proposed treatment plan.
- The means by which a referral outside the practice may be facilitated most comfortably for the patient.
- If treatment is to continue within the practice by the counsellor, or jointly with the GP, the nature/style of the work, the frequency of the sessions and the length of the contract.
- If the practice is a fund-holding practice and an outside referral is necessary, the willingness of the GP to fund treatment for the patient.

Counselling options

A number of possible treatment options are available to the counsellor.

Brief therapy

Brief therapy or time-limited therapy usually means somewhere between six and twelve sessions. However, brief therapy may also include a more flexible arrangement where patients are seen for counselling over a relatively short period of time, or where the frequency of sessions is adapted to the individual needs of the patient. Whichever form of brief therapy is adopted, it is usually appropriate for those patients with a specific problem that requires focused help, for example a sudden loss or bereavement, such as the death of a partner or family member, a pregnancy termination or miscarriage, loss of employment/redundancy or the breakdown of a relationship or marriage.

CASE EXAMPLE: MR JOHNSON

An anxious, 55 year old, high-powered business man comes to see the counsellor after being warned by a heart specialist that he must reduce his workload and lose weight as he is at risk of a heart attack. Initially he is sceptical about the value of counselling, but realises during two assessment interviews that his anger with his father for taking him away from his mother at a young age has left him with a ruthless, controlling attitude towards his wife and children, other women and his colleagues at work. He agrees to six sessions of brief therapy with the counsellor to focus on his suppressed anger and the effect it is having on his body, his mind and his relationships.

Longer-term counselling or therapy

Although some counsellors work for two or three days a week within a practice, and we know of one counsellor who is employed on a full-time basis, for the most part counsellors are rarely able to contemplate regular, extended therapeutic work in a primary care setting – long-term treatment will require referrals to local NHS psychotherapy services or to private counsellors or therapists in the area. The indications that longer-term counselling or psychotherapy will be beneficial are when the patient shows signs that he or she is likely to become very dependent on the counsellor and when there is evidence of early trauma or abandonment in the patient's family history. It is generally true to say that the earlier the roots of the damage, the more likely the patient is to benefit from the regularity and containment of longer-term, intensive treatment.

CASE EXAMPLE: MRS HART

Mrs Hart, a young woman in her early thirties, comes to see the counsellor for therapy as she cannot stay in any one job and is depressed after a third relationship with a man has collapsed because she is frightened of intimacy. She is obviously able and creative, but feels that she sabotages any possibility of using her talents. Her father was physically and sexually abusive and her mother was unable to protect herself or her children from his violence. The patient left home at seventeen to travel the world and settled in England, where she got a good job she could not enjoy. She sees the counsellor for three assessment interviews and the counsellor recommends long-term psychotherapy. She refers herself as a training patient to one of the subsidised schemes available from a psychotherapy training organisation.

Supportive counselling'

There are a great number of patients who can benefit from occasional, supportive sessions, spread over a longer period of time. Some patients may need to be seen once every few weeks over a two-year period, sometimes for only half an hour. These may include elderly patients who are struggling with problems of loneliness, reduced physical capacity or loss of loved ones. It may also be helpful for those psychiatric patients who are kept stable with regular medication but need help with day-to-day life issues and emotional problems. When patients have suffered intense bereavement reactions that have triggered off earlier losses, ongoing support over a period of time is also likely to be helpful.

CASE EXAMPLE: MRS MCKENZIE SMITH

A 78 year old depressed woman presents to the counsellor after her husband has died after a long illness, throughout which she cared for him. It was an unhappy marriage and she feels he forced her to live for many years in a house she hated. Although she claims not to miss him, she finds herself unable to 'do anything' and has retreated from her family and friends into the dark interior of the hated house. The counsellor gradually encourages her to talk about herself and her personal background, and realises that the combined effect of her bereavement and finding herself isolated in this house has recreated the dark, barren atmosphere of her early childhood – her mother died when she was very young. She suggests to the patient that they meet every few weeks as a way of providing ego-support for the part of her that wants to find a new, lighter flat and build a different life for herself.

Shared care

Plans involving shared work/management of the patient by the counsellor and GP are most effective for difficult patients with a long history of visits to the practice and of multiple relationships with different members of the primary health care team. Patients with entrenched psychosomatic problems and those with person-ality problems come to mind here. Regular sessions with the GP and counsellor, providing both can work satisfactorily together, are likely to offer patients a unique opportunity for joint work, which contains them and can lead to real progress. Part of the success of this work involves facilitating a shift of emphasis in the GP's mind from 'cure', which is unlikely to be possible, towards a belief that allowing the patient to use the practice regularly as a containing, safe place will allow him or her to make the best use of the limited resources in the practice and in his or her life.

CASE EXAMPLE: MR BASUDI

Mr Basudi, a single, Middle-Eastern man in his sixties, comes to see the counsellor, ostensibly because of his housing difficulties. He has been forced to remain in a run-down flat with a difficult landlord who refuses to make any necessary improvements, and with neighbours who are noisy, abusive and constantly invade his space. He has various physical complaints and is recovering from a serious cancer operation. He wants the counsellor to write a letter to the housing department supporting his request to be rehoused on physical and emotional grounds. After a consultation with the referring GP, the counsellor tells the patient that the GP will write on his behalf to the local authorities and suggests he arrange regular (containing) visits to the GP to monitor his physical condition. The counsellor offers him occasional sessions to discuss ways in which he can develop some of his interests and relationships as a way of helping him to manage his housing difficulties. The counsellor and GP agree to meet every so often to review the situation.

Individual, group, marital or family work?

It is probably true to say that most counsellors working in primary care are most comfortable doing individual, one-to-one work. However there are real opportunities within a practice to carry out group, family or marital work. We know of counsellors running short-term, focused groups and longer-term, less structured, more analytically orientated groups within a practice. Examples of the former are groups for mothers with young children, groups for displaced people from other cultures, women's groups and groups for patients with eating disorders. Given that the counsellor has sufficient time, training and interest, a longer-term group where patients may come and go for periods of time can also be an effective use of resources.

Specialised training in marital work would be of great benefit to many counsellors working in primary care. A first assessment session with a new patient often reveals a marital problem and the possibility of a valuable short-term intervention with both partners. In some cases it may be difficult for GPs to intervene if both husband and wife are on the practice list and demand individual confidentiality. A counsellor who sees one partner is likely to find it easier to suggest that the other partner might like to come as well, and the assessment can progress from there. Many counsellors are wary of marital work, but there is good evidence to suggest that couple therapy can be effective in a relatively short space of time (see the case example of the Locks in Chapter 6).

Summary

It will be evident to the reader that the role of the counsellor working in a primary care setting is likely to be comprehensive. Assessment is a fundamental part of the counsellor's role and the more experience, training and supervision the counsellor finds for him or herself in this area, the better.

Assessing a patient in a primary care setting provides an opportunity for some good work to be done at an early stage. Visiting the GP is likely to be the first thing patients do when they have an emotional problem. To see a counsellor on the premises, with the support of the GP, may prevent some problems from becoming chronic and also offer patients a chance of relief, or at least short-term relief, with the minimum of delay.

This chapter has highlighted how an assessment must take account not only of the patient, but also of the setting, in particular what is going on in the GP's mind when deciding to refer some patients for assessment whilst not referring others. The assessment interview(s) may be described as a microcosm of the patient's life and probably also of any subsequent counselling or therapy he or she may choose. Many patients are likely to remember the event for many years and the dynamics of the interview(s) are usually a good predictor of the path of any future therapy. The responsibility of the assessor to get close enough to the patient to get in touch with his or her unconscious processes whilst sustaining sufficient distance to think about what is happening, is considerable.

This chapter has tried to illustrate the excitement of the assessment interview described by Holmes (1995) and Coltart (1993), and also to confirm the emotional power of the assessment situation, which can mask many of the difficulties in the 'here and now' of the process itself. Assessing in primary care will inevitably produce a collision between opposing unconscious forces and it demands Janus-like, simultaneous attention to a number of different perspectives. For the assessor working in a GP practice, pressure on the gate-keeping process is likely to come in the form of an excessive number of referrals and political pressure in an atmosphere of scarce resources. These however are visible, the sentry can see them coming, and a vigilant external sentry/management function is crucial. However the dynamics within the practice and the transference/counter-transference relationship with the patient are likely to present the assessor with the possibility of more subtle, insidious influences on his or her therapeutic integrity, which are more likely to require a vigilant internal sentry function.

6

ONGOING WORK IN PRIMARY CARE

A psychodynamic approach towards ongoing work

All counsellors who work in a primary health care environment hold a body of knowledge, the content of which is likely to have been influenced by their training and personal therapy, and will in turn influence their beliefs about their work, theoretically, clinically and morally. The models of the mind that affect the ways in which we work and think are also affected and modified by new experiences in life in general as well as through clinical practice. Both authors, albeit trained in institutions with a different orientation (Freudian and Jungian), subscribe to what might be called a *psychodynamic approach* when working in primary care. We support Bateman and Holmes' (1995) three central moral tenets of psychoanalysis, which have become incorporated into present-day social and political debate. These have clear relevance to relationships within primary care. They are (1) the high value placed upon *truth*, with all the personal pain this may involve; (2) the link between *good nurturing experiences in childhood* and a well-functioning society; and (3) *the value of autonomy* in its own right, which may develop out of sensitive parenting. Whether or not readers are sympathetic to these beliefs, an important question that must be raised here is whether we are practising psychoanalysis in our work in primary care.

What exactly are we doing?

Freud said that he was not really interested in treating ill people, but was excited about the value of psychoanalysis as an investigative technique with which to explore the workings of the human psyche, particularly when he could see people several times a week. His research was motivated by his committed enthusiasm to this new method, and his Viennese patients seemed willing to try to work in the ways he asked of them. However in primary care we *are* treating ill people, who come to us because they want to feel better. There are many more patients asking for help than we have the resources to treat and we certainly do not see them several times a week. Whilst the methods we use are most important, and we have to recognise that contemporary forms of psychodynamic therapy have evolved from Freud and Jung's seminal work, the primary care environment does not allow us the luxury of the purist adherence to a single-minded technique that is possible in private practice. There must be adaptation, and as we have emphasised throughout this book, counselling placements are most likely to be successful if counsellors can work flexibly in the busy atmosphere of the 'souk' (see Chapter 1). The question then arises of how we may understand and think about the nature of ongoing work that takes place in the surgery. Coltart finds psychotherapy easier than psychoanalysis:

> dynamic psychotherapy seems to me to keep one at full stretch all the time; although people are capable of surprising one indefinitely, and unexpected flashes of thought and insight certainly arise during the course of an analysis, the very classicism of the container means there is less scope for adventures of the spirit. (Coltart, 1993, p. 18).

This quotation provides a good description of counselling work in primary care, in particular the term 'adventures of the spirit', although it is not clear whether this has more relevance for us as counsellors and GPs learning to work together or for the patients we are trying to treat! The term 'adventure' embodies the idea of some kind of journey for the participants and an ongoing process, surely two of the main elements of a psychodynamic approach to counselling. The word 'spirit', as used by Coltart, seems to convey a sense of body *and* mind, of trying out new things, making the most of what is available and the possibility of freshness and spontaneity in counselling relationships. In our work in the practice we do apply elements of the 'classicism of the [intellectual] container', since it is difficult for any work to take place unless it is within thoughtfully established boundaries, involving a safe, quiet and private place in which to work, careful timekeeping and so on. This safeguards a space in which the counselling relationship may evolve with integrity. However the variety of patients who are seen and the opportunities for teamwork and collaborative activities with the

GPs mean that whilst an 'analytical attitude' to the activities that take place in the surgery is invaluable, a steadfast and rigid application of psychoanalytic principles and techniques to all counselling work is unlikely to prove successful. Counselling in primary care has distinctive features, unique to its context, drawing on some of the principles of psychoanalysis whilst not necessarily putting them all into practice.

In this chapter we illustrate the range of 'adventures of the spirit' and the variety of approaches to ongoing, day-to-day work by using a number of different case examples, and in the discussion that follows each example we incorporate some of the psychodynamic thinking that underpins our approach to clinical work. The reader is encouraged to refer to Appendix A at the end of the book for a review of relevant psychodynamic and other concepts.

Struggles towards teamwork

CASE EXAMPLE: THE MARTINS

The Martins – Mr and Mrs Martin and their son Sebastian – are a middle-class family who have all been registered with the practice for some years. Mrs Martin has become increasingly concerned about her son's behaviour. Sebastian, aged 35, worked in the City but had been finding it increasingly difficult to concentrate at work and was asked to leave. He had started to behave very strangely: he had lost what ability he had to communicate and was visiting prostitutes as he could not find a girlfriend. He appeared to hear what was being asked of him but could not respond in a coherent way.

In the first instance it is a very agitated Mrs Martin who comes to discuss her son's condition with the GP. The GP asks to see Sebastian and is puzzled about what might be wrong with him. Sebastian is polite and eager to please, but incoherent and virtually monosyllabic in his responses to questions about his well-being. He expresses the view that if only he could find a girlfriend everything would be better. The GP wonders whether his symptoms might suggest the onset of a (schizophrenic) breakdown or whether they could signify an organic brain disease. He decides to refer Sebastian to the practice counsellor for a psychological assessment and second opinion before taking any further action.

The counsellor sees Sebastian for three sessions in an effort to discover whether there might be any psychological reasons for his regression. She too finds it extremely difficult to communicate with him: 'it is as if he has no self, all he can do is to mirror back to me what I am saying to him'. She begins to realise, however, that this is an enmeshed family where Sebastian and his mother are strongly (ambivalently?) attached to each other. After a concerned discussion with the GP, they decide on a brain scan and other organic tests for Sebastian in order to eliminate the possibility of organic disease. While waiting for the brain scan Sebastian, encouraged by his parents, visits two different private psychiatrists, each of whom makes a different psychiatric diagnosis. Eventually he is referred to the consultant psychiatrist at the local NHS hospital for a psychiatric and psychological assessment.

After some weeks the GP asks the counsellor if she will consider seeing Mrs Martin, who is 'angry and anxious' about what is happening at the local psychiatric unit. The counsellor agrees and finds herself having to work hard to contain a potentially explosive situation. The unit is taking a long time to assess Sebastian, and wishes to admit him for observation as he is a difficult case to diagnose. She is worried about the effect on Sebastian of mixing with 'mad people in the hospital', and she has failed in her attempt to discuss the situation with the consultant. Her telephone calls have not been answered and on the only occasion she and her husband met the consultant, he could only spare them five minutes. She told the counsellor that Sebastian was getting worse, that her husband was no help and that she must bear most of the anxiety and push for action to be taken. Mr Martin had an accident a few years previously and the head injury he suffered has affected his capacity to take responsibility for matters in the household.

The counsellor, who is no longer seeing Sebastian, decides to offer Mrs Martin occasional sessions every few weeks (all she could manage with a busy schedule) in a general attempt to contain the situation and give Mrs Martin a place to air her feelings during the stressful wait for a diagnosis. She discovers that Mrs Martin herself has a complicated medical history and has recently had breast cancer.

The assessment procedure at the hospital is indeed lengthy and both GP and counsellor become angry with the consultant and his team. The GP complains to the consultant (who also happens to be his patient at the surgery!) Eventually, after some months, when emotions are running very high, the psychiatric unit decides to hold a case conference to discuss Sebastian and the family situation. Those present are the consultant, a senior psychiatric nurse who has been observing Sebastian, the psychology team carrying out cognitive and personality tests, a family therapist who is working with the family, plus the GP and the counsellor from the practice. During the discussion it is agreed that extensive and repeated tests have revealed no organic damage. The psychologist considers that Sebastian is intelligent but severely emotionally damaged, like a regressed, helpless child. It is agreed that the family is extremely enmeshed and that the only hope for Sebastian's improvement is to try to help him separate from his mother by leaving the family home, moving initially into some sort of protected environment where appropriate therapies (supportive initially) are available. The family are then invited to join the meeting, but the consultant has to leave after ten minutes following an emergency telephone call. The meeting becomes difficult. Sebastian and Mr Martin withdraw into silence, and Mrs Martin looks explosive and is barely able to contain her anger at the consultant's departure. The outcome of the meeting is that the family therapy will continue and an attempt will be made to find a place for Sebastian in a Richmond Fellowship hostel. The GP practice is encouraged to continue to support Mrs Martin.

The counsellor likes Mrs Martin and goes on working with her. Sebastian continues to regress but remains at home, where his mother cares for him with some minimal support from her husband. Sebastian starts to see the practice community nurse after the (much loved) family therapist leaves the local hospital.

The Martins still feel angry and disappointed about their treatment at the local NHS hospital and are discouraged that no-one has managed to provide any 'useful medical or psychological help' for Sebastian. They do not want Sebastian to go into a Richmond Fellowship hostel as it will not be the 'right' environment for him. They ask the GP for a second referral, and in the GP's words he then sends them to the 'best person for this in the country'. Sebastian goes through another lengthy assessment process lasting several months at a second hospital, which similarly finds no organic damage and diagnoses an emotional disorder of the self, brought on by the failure of Sebastian and his parents, particularly his mother, to separate.

Eventually Sebastian does manage to spend some nights away from his parents in a next-door flat run by a voluntary religious organisation. The GP looking after the family leaves to join another practice and the psychiatric nurse threatens to stop her sessions with Sebastian as they are 'not getting anywhere'.

A new GP joins the practice and takes over the medical care of the Martins. He consults the counsellor, who feels it is now time to make some boundaries for this family, as it is evident that neither Sebastian nor his parents can, as yet, live apart. They arrive at the joint view that the best way forward will be to try to contain the family within the practice and that a policy of 'managing the situation' will be pursued. A family discussion is arranged, to which the old and new GPs, the psychiatric nurse, the counsellor and the family are invited. The family are told that this is a situation with which they must now live and that there are to be no further referrals for assessment or treatment. The new GP expresses his view that the prognosis for Sebastian is not very good, but that Sebastian may continue to receive supportive counselling from the psychiatric nurse. The counsellor will continue to work with Mrs Martin on an occasional basis. The focus will be on helping her to accept her son's illness and on trying to separate from him sufficiently for her to have some life of her own. All three professionals agree to set up regular meetings to review the situation.

Psychodynamically, this is a family where the son failed to negotiate the oedipal situation and began to break down when his already fragile male identity/ego was threatened by the loss of his job and a failure to form successful relationships. A strong, possessive mother and a weak father who was unable to break up the mother–son couple was a particularly difficult combination for the son, which may have allowed Sebastian to internalise a parental couple who were separate and whom he felt (unconsciously) that he could control. While consciously he wanted a girlfriend, unconsciously he was terrified to replace his mother, who was unlikely adequately to have met his emotional needs in childhood. It may be that visiting prostitutes was a way of denigrating the women he felt so ambivalent about.

The Martins were a powerful, demanding family where many of the denied, inexpressible, angry feelings were split off and projected into the helpers, who then experienced the anger. Mrs Martin unconsciously divided her helpers into the 'good' (GP, counsellor, family therapist) and the 'bad' (consultant, psychologist). These positive and negative transferences are another example of splitting. She and Mr Martin repeatedly denied the seriousness of their son's illness and Mrs Martin even produced a variety of somatic symptoms. Sebastian's gradual withdrawal from many aspects of ordinary life suggest a 'defence of the self' (Fordham, 1985), where his symptoms were an unconscious attempt to protect himself from extreme pain and anxiety that were often of psychotic proportions.

An enmeshed family like this, where one family member is ill, difficult to diagnose and fails to improve, challenges the aims of primary care to make people better. Agreeing to a series of referrals to several different specialists could be seen as collusion on behalf of the practice staff to avoid facing the painful reality of their helplessness. Both the GP and the counsellor became angry with the slow and inefficient NHS psychiatric unit and failed to take containing action early enough because they did not give themselves sufficient space to stand back and reflect upon the ways in which the family was unconsciously affecting them. The prolonged assessment process and the difficulty in trusting the opinion of experienced professionals seem to have functioned for both family and professionals as a way of avoiding painful truths and facing difficult realities. The splits operating within the family were played out in the practice, where the old GP and the counsellor could be said to have avoided facing realities too. Both could be said to have become identified with the 'saviour' projections from the family.

It is only when there was an injection of new blood and a new GP joined the practice as a firm parent that some change became possible. The several instances of 'departures' – when the consultant left early, the old GP left, the family therapist left, and the psychiatric nurse threatened to stop her work with Sebastian – suggest that the professionals were acting out what was most difficult for this family – allowing each other to function as separate individuals.

In systemic terms, the boundaries, power relationships and conscious and unconscious agendas within this family and between the family and the professionals involved present a challenge to our beliefs about effective teamwork. The 'positive feedback' (see Appendix A) in this system was to do with an understandable collective fantasy that Sebastian could return to his former self and thus ensure the continuing homeostasis/equilibrium of the family system. It was only when the family and the staff in the practice were able to cope with 'negative feedback', largely triggered by the appearance of the new GP into the practice, that change could happen. He found it easier than the other professionals involved to acknowledge the need for a change from a model of 'cure' to one of 'adapting to realities of the situation', so that some transformation could occur and the family and professionals could begin to accept and adapt to their difficulties.

Counselling and ethnicity

Ethnicity is a factor in the patient–counsellor relationship even when both are members of the same ethnic group. Ethnic patients may feel alien in a strange culture, even if their family and cultural ties are strong. Some ethnic groups are suspicious of Western medicine, others display an unhelpful dependency on it. Anxieties about separateness, cultural integration, assimilation, loss of identity, pride in their social group or religion, or shame about being part of a minority group may all have bearing on how patients relate to their doctors and counsellors. Some may see their doctor as a god-like figure who can solve everything. Others may rely on somatisation of their personal and social conflicts, because they do not understand them or feel they cannot do much about them. Internalising the conflict as a physical symptom may be easier than talking about feelings, family problems, religion or culture. Shame, disloyalty and fear of ostracism may combine with the feeling that the doctor will not understand the problem anyway, or may harbour prejudices about the patient's culture. These phenomena may make patients repeatedly turn up at the surgery with various symptoms. As counsellors we may easily miss the core conflicts from which our patients suffer, partly through ignorance and partly through fear of revealing our own prejudices. This may lead us artificially to overcompensate in order to demonstrate how accepting we are of other people's differences.

CASE EXAMPLE: NINA

Nina, an East-African Moslem woman of 50, tells the counsellor of her difficulty in handling her angry feelings towards her husband and her deceased father. Her doctor had detected her conflict and spoken to her about it. She expressed concern to him about her persistent angry feelings and he suggested she speak to the counsellor. She is not sure whether her anger is caused by changes in her husband's employment situation, or whether he has become the target of anger originally directed at her father. The current trigger of her emotions, she says, is the failure of her husband's business ventures, but she has felt anger for a long time – ever since she was married off according to religious tradition at 18 by her father to a man she had never met before. Her likes and dislikes, her interests and ambitions were not taken into account. She resolved to do the right thing by turning herself into a dutiful wife and a good mother. She feels that she was successful at this until her husband badly misjudged certain business deals, lost all his money and became depressed and apathetic. He could not, or would not, recover and she then resolved to follow her own path of personal fulfilment, which she had suspended when she married. She withdrew from her husband emotionally and sexually, made sure that her children were properly established in their careers and decided to travel abroad.

She returns from time to time to the marital home, lives in it with her husband, but is preparing herself via courses of study and assiduous financial management to lead an independent life, which may or may not include her husband. At times, she feels alone and even a little guilty about what she is doing. The patient is pleased to have the opportunity to talk about her problems, especially as anger is an emotion in which Moslem women are not supposed 'to indulge'. Talking about it is providing her with a sense of relief, as is the encouragement she is receiving to think about herself and her life.

The counsellor was aware of the tension caused by the patient's inner struggles for emancipation, and the conflict she experienced between Western individualism and Eastern collectivism. He refrained from being too openly supportive of her wish for personal fulfilment or too critical of the repressive aspects of her culture. A neutral approach, a space for thinking, was what the patient needed and this was available in the surgery. The patient attended three sessions, after which she said that she had benefited from talking to the counsellor and considering the various options open to her. She also felt more tolerant of her husband, which in turn increased his self-confidence. She found herself liking him more and he began to emerge from his depression.

CASE EXAMPLE: NASEEM

Naseem is a 29 year old Asian woman in great physical pain following a car accident. She is also depressed, lethargic and self-critical. The accident and its aftermath have upset her precarious balance of personal functioning. She had several personal problems prior to the accident, which probably account for her depression. She has a long-standing, difficult and sometimes violent relationship with her boyfriend and her flat has been repossessed for non-payment of the mortgage. She tells the counsellor how she felt neglected by her family during adolescence because of her flirtations with boys and her wish to enjoy the youth culture around her. She was angry with them for their apparent old-fashioned conservatism and they were disappointed with her because she had turned her back on traditional values. Far from finding a new and stable independence, Naseem grew more anxious, guilty and self-deprecating, which she compensated for with a flouncy, precocious bubbliness.

Her manic denials and querulous complaints about others make it difficult to engage with her psychologically. The counsellor grows tired of her accusations and obsessive disappointment in everyone. She is late for her three counselling sessions, explaining her lateness in terms of the vicissitudes of others and expressing surprise that she has to have shortened sessions. She persists in talking excitedly and the counsellor feels that she is competing with him, arguing about the comments and interpretations he gives her. The patient seems so vehement in her complaints that the counsellor is prevented from intervening, but at the same time pressurised to do so. Naseem says she feels resentful because the insurance company, the other driver, her boyfriend and the building society have all tried to show how superior they are, which makes her feel naive and gullible. The counsellor comments on her envy and how she tries to defend herself by feeling victimised and blaming others for her predicaments. The patient's response is to become calmer and she seems capable of some self-awareness.

The counsellor works with her painful, bitter, envious experiences and later the patient says she has remembered his comments about her tendency to place responsibility for her predicament on others, and this has helped her to be less argumentative. Over the three weeks of the counselling sessions, Naseem takes a hard look at herself and begins to feel much better. Her joints become more supple, her pain diminishes and she says she feels stronger within herself.

Lacking support from within her own ethnic group, Naseem's agenda was to build allies from the dominant culture. The counsellor's refusal to collude with her surface problems led her to examine her deeper conflicts and ultimately to a better understanding and sympathetic response to her own roots, as well as an appreciation of her place in society as a whole. This patient's identification with her ethnic group had weakened without her having developed correspondingly stronger links to her dominant culture. She participated in the consumerist technological society, yet was not properly part of it. The anomie of urban society had affected her and she was troubled by family discord, alcohol-related problems and minor criminal behaviour.

In this case the counsellor's interventions were directed at Naseem's fantasy of keeping the real world of relationships distant and remaining unconscious of what was really going on in her internal world of feelings and emotions. Her rather glib declaration that all her troubles were the fault of others made for a difficult therapeutic encounter. However, as a result of the counsellor's perseverance the patient began a process of reflection and she came to see her own contribution to some of her difficulties. In a sad tone, she remarked that the counsellor could understand and comment on her feelings about her drive to be 'someone' in the world of the dominant culture, but in reality he was part of that culture and she was on the periphery. This insight had helped her, she said, to be more tolerant of her own culture, to be less driven to win and to reconsider how she discharged her personal and social obligations.

Neither author has had any special training in counselling work with patients from other cultures, though both are descendants of immigrants and have personal experience of and an interest in the problem of adjusting to life in a culture that is not the culture of origin. The majority of counsellors working in the field may be in this or a similar situation. Whether or not this matters is a subject for debate, but the skill for GPs and counsellors alike is to be sufficiently attentive to cultural factors and their social implications, as well as the more usual inter- and intrapersonal dynamics.

Revisiting the practice: 'the revolving door'

Near-immediate availability of medical services is the hallmark of the British primary care system. Most registered patients can simply turn up at the surgery and wait to be seen by a GP. Not so with counselling. Counselling services are structured by appointment systems and fixed-length interviews. Anyone needing urgent attention from a counsellor will have to wait. In spite of these differences between the ways in which doctors and counsellors organise and use their time, some aspects of the character of their respective services and the way they are managed will inevitably come to resemble each other. For example, on the whole patients know intuitively when their symptoms can no longer be dealt with by aspirin and rest and require a visit to the doctor. On average patients visit their doctors about six times a year. They come and go and it can be said that in between visits the 'doctoring' that is necessary to sustain reasonable health is undertaken personally by each individual in his or her own way.

This is also the case with counselling. Many patients who have emotional difficulties or are stressed may have between one and six sessions with the counsellor, after which they may feel better, a problem is resolved, a life decision made and so on, and further counselling sessions may not be necessary. The 'open door' or 'revolving door' principle of medical availability applies, with some differences, to counselling too. This is the character of primary care and one of its main strengths is fairly prompt attention to most ailments and referral to specialists for more serious problems. Patients feel contained by this system and practitioners feel comfortable too, knowing that their patients will return to them if their condition worsens or they become worried. Consequently the doctor–patient relationship evolves slowly. Patients reveal as much or as little about themselves as they wish. GPs hear about their patients' life events and difficulties at different times and there can be an easy-come, easy-go aspect to these relationships. The following case illustrates the patch-and-mend character of primary care in a patient's contact with her GP and counsellor.

CASE EXAMPLE: CAROL

Fifty year old Carol comes to her GP in a state of panic. She is hyperventilating and tearful. A 15 minute chat with her GP makes her feel better and she is referred to the counsellor, who sees her within three days. Carol tells the counsellor that she believes her stress is work-related. She is a carer for the elderly and latterly her managers have made excessive demands on her, refusing to listen to her assertion that the work can not be done with the existing resources. Carol's high standards of professional care mean that she is driving herself hard to try to achieve impossible targets. The counsellor suggests that the bottleneck at work may be mirrored physically in the 'bottleneck' in her breathing. Carol reflects on this and tells the counsellor how she has always tried to do a good job and do what her mother has wanted. Mostly she has succeeded, but there is something at work that has simply 'stuck in her throat' and she has had enough. She talks about her early life, her marriage and divorce, and the child she brought up alone. This too she did successfully and with pride. Her commitment and abilities are acknowledged by the counsellor and Carol feels better for talking. One further appointment is arranged and it covers much the same ground. Carol is grateful for the support she has received but says she does not need any more counselling.

Eighteen months later Carol returns to see her doctor with sleeping problems, mild anxiety and depression. She is again referred to the counsellor, who senses that this time Carol is more seriously depressed, almost suicidal. Carol once more turns the conversation to her unhelpful and unfeeling managers, but the counsellor suggests that she may also be talking about feeling uncared for personally and she is probably struggling with anxieties about her age and an increasing sense of uselessness. She cries and says that all her efforts to do good and to be loved for it have amounted to nothing. Menopausal symptoms are making her feel that she has little to look forward to. She is lonely and does little to protect herself. When criticised, she readily takes the blame. This session concentrates on strategies that she might use at work to address the bullying of which she is a victim. She appears to gain immediate emotional strength from the discussion.

In the session a fortnight later, Carol explains how she has initiated a series of steps with her employers to look into her working conditions and her relationship with her managers. She says that if things did not turn out satisfactorily, she will not feel bound to stay on in her job. She has skills and is still employable elsewhere. She will not put all her eggs in one basket. She feels more confident and assertive and no further appointments are made.

This is a good example of the 'revolving door' phenomenon in primary care. Many areas in Carol's life could have been opened for discussion, but she had not come for that. The sessions were focused, goal-oriented and directive. She felt supported, relieved and motivated. Her symptoms abated and she gained the strength to fight the battles at work. The nature of primary care is predicated on a model of 'how little need we do?', rather than 'how much must we do?' Concise, focused comments set Carol on her way. They did not transform her personality; instead they dealt with an immediate issue. If and when further problems arise, the surgery team will be available to help Carol again. Revisiting the counsellor in this setting is easier and more accessible than referral to private practice or specialist clinics.

Working with couples: who has the problem?

CASE EXAMPLE: THE LOCKS

Mrs Lock is a likeable, thoughtful Spanish woman of 35 who comes to talk to the counsellor about her loss of interest in sex with her husband since the birth of their first child a few months previously. She puts this down to the sexual abuse that occurred in her family: her father and at least two of her brothers had abused two of her sisters and, to a lesser extent, Mrs Lock herself. She uses the first two sessions with the counsellor to explore how the birth of her child and her anxieties about her role as a parent have reawakened memories of traumatic intrusions from the male members of her family, with little or no protection of the children by their mother. It is the first time that she has spoken to anyone about these events. There is then a holiday break, and when Mrs Lock returns for a third session she tells the counsellor that she feels better. She has been to Spain and has begun to have conversations with her sisters and one of her brothers about what happened in their childhood. These are helping her to feel less of a victim and more able to deal with the present problems in her own marriage. She confesses to the counsellor that her husband has severe obsessional symptoms that are exhausting her and she is annoyed that he seems unable to take any responsibility for finding help for himself. The counsellor asks Mrs Lock whether she would like her husband to attend another session with her. She agrees to ask him and they attend the next session together.

It emerges that Mr Lock is himself the victim of abuse – physical rather than sexual. He is the eldest son of a family with a strong, sometimes physically violent mother and a father, a painter, who shut himself off from family problems. Mr Lock was bullied at school and remembers being very unhappy when his parents did not allow him to leave. He developed obsessional symptoms from the age of thirteen, beginning with compulsive hand washing and later generalising into intense phobic symptoms about anything connected with his family.

Mrs Lock is particularly upset about her husband's behaviour when she returns from work each afternoon. Mrs Lock works with Mr Lock's sister, and because of this family connection he never lets his wife pick up their baby until she has washed her hands and changed her clothes. For the past two years he has not allowed Mrs Lock to drive their car as he feels she will 'pollute' the steering wheel. Whenever he drives anywhere near his parent's home he becomes anxious and obsessional and needs to find another route. Mrs Lock tries to be tolerant about his symptoms and accommodate his wishes, but she is running out of patience and is seriously worried about the effect their personal problems will have on the emotional development of their baby.

After one session alone with Mr Lock and three further joint sessions, the counsellor reviews the present situation with the couple and possible routes forward. Mr Lock is ambivalent about finding personal help for his obsessions and the counsellor wonders about the degree of aggression and violence that underlie his present symptoms. He has rejected two previous offers of help, one by a local, private clinical psychologist, whom he claims not to have liked, and the second by the local NHS outpatient psychotherapy clinic, where he failed to attend his assessment interview. The counsellor decides to continue to see them once every few weeks as a couple. Both attend, and after several sessions Mr Lock agrees to a referral to the local psychology department for assessment to see whether longer-term psychotherapy or a more behavioural approach to his symptoms would be most helpful. The couple wish to continue their occasional sessions with the practice counsellor in order to work on their marital difficulties, particularly Mr Lock's demand that his wife accommodate his symptoms and Mrs. Lock's loss of interest in their sexual relationship.

Mrs Lock went to see the counsellor with a double agenda. Consciously, she wanted help to process powerful memories and feelings that were intruding into her present life, arising from events in her childhood. It is not unusual for such memories to unfold at the birth of a child and for women who have been the victims of sexual abuse to project many of their fears into their own children out of unconscious anxiety that the abuse will be reenacted in the next generation. Less consciously however, Mrs Lock wanted the counsellor to see Mr Lock and encourage him to find help for his personal difficulties. Although she loved her husband and wished their marriage to last, she was angry about his emotional 'abuse' of her freedom to hold and cuddle her baby whenever she wanted.

Although Mr Lock attended the first two joint sessions reluctantly, his one session alone with the counsellor seemed to help him to feel less threatened by the counsellor and to face the seriousness of his obsessional disorder and its possible effects on his marriage and his daughter, both of whom he loved. Referral outside the practice, while still retaining joint sessions of marital work within the practice, seemed to be an offer from a flexible rather than a punitive and unbending parent, as was the case in his childhood. It was therefore one he could accept rather than reject, as had happened previously.

Many counsellors working in a primary care setting are not trained to work with couples, and yet a good proportion of individual patients who visit counsellors for an assessment bring problems that suggest the partner's involvement is the natural next step. The counsellor working with the Locks had had no special training in couple work, but over time, and with experience and growing confidence, she took on the work as a new 'adventure of the spirit'. Mixed therapies, as in the case above, involving both individual and couple work in the practice, as well as referral to an outside agency, are the bread and butter of counselling referrals in primary care. Counsellors with supervision and the possibility of supplementary training, may need to journey beyond their original training into less familiar waters if they are to provide treatment that is truly in the best interests of the patients registered with the surgery.

Brief therapy: a life audit

CASE EXAMPLE: ROBERT

Robert is in his early forties and comes to see the counsellor because he is feeling 'stuck' in his life and believes that he is underachieving. Since the break-up of his marriage two years previously he has lived alone, 'in retreat' as he puts it, and apart from two regular though unrewarding jobs and occasional meetings with his two daughters his life feels empty. He is depressed and has been on Prozac for a few months. He is quite insightful about himself and his difficulties and has had both individual and group therapy in the past for long-standing obsessional problems. His mother died after a long illness when he was thirteen and he was then brought up by his father, who drank heavily, and his two older sisters, under the supervision of a strict and humourless aunt. He tells the counsellor that when he gets involved with a woman he becomes preoccupied with obsessive thoughts about her past sexual relationships.

After two assessment interviews Robert and the counsellor agree to meet for six sessions, one every three or four weeks, to focus on the gap that exists between his ideals for himself and the reality of what he can achieve. He finds the sessions give him the confidence to continue this quest, and realises that 'small steps' rather than 'huge changes' are more realistic. When their sessions are over, they review the situation and Robert asks to be referred for group psychotherapy, in the hope that this will help him live more comfortably with his depression and obsessional symptoms, while continuing to pursue a career and new relationships.

Some reference to brief therapy has already been made in Chapter 5. In the above case example, the counsellor assessed Robert, a patient with long-standing emotional/psychiatric problems but who clearly had a fairly well-functioning ego and the capacity to hold down jobs and make relationships. Although he was depressed, he was insightful about some of the reasons for his state of mind as he had had previous therapy. He was not in a position to pay for private individual counselling as he gave a proportion of his earnings to his ex-wife to help with the care and maintenance of his daughters. He showed evidence of having learned to manage his symptoms except when depressed, when he became self-critical and his internal 'strict aunt', a reflection of the aunt who took over his care after the early death of his mother, began to persecute him by telling him that he was underachieving and worthless.

The counsellor was not in a position to offer him the long-term support he probably needed, but could offer a limited number of sessions to carry out a 'life audit', an opportunity to review his situation again, to reinforce what he really knew. Managing his life was likely to be easier with ongoing professional support to give him the confidence to test reality in a limited way, rather than staying in the grip of his idealised and unattainable fantasies as a manic defence against his depression.

Supportive counselling: 'asking for what you need'

CASE EXAMPLE: MRS SIMPSON

Mrs Simpson is an intelligent and cultured woman of 63. She comes to see the counsellor in a very anxious and depressed state with a number of somatic symptoms after her husband has left her to set up home with another woman. She is self-contained and does not talk easily about her feelings. Because her marriage had been unhappy for some years she is surprised that she is reacting so strongly. She feels betrayed by two of her four children, who had not told her of her husband's infidelity. During the course of three assessment interviews she comes to see that her feeling of abandonment is in part a reenactment of an earlier trauma, when she had felt her mother had not liked her and had emotionally abandoned her. At the time she had felt pushed out into the cold, and she thinks that this has probably contributed to her impression on others as a cold and distant person. She never knew her father and is an only child.

Mrs Simpson's capacity for psychodynamic work is immediately evident and she and the counsellor discuss the possibility of a referral outside the practice for private analytical psychotherapy. She even visits a psychotherapist, but decides that this is not what she wants. She returns to see the counsellor, who asks what help she would like. Mrs Simpson says she realises the counsellor can not see her regularly, but that as they have made good contact she thinks it will suit her well to see her once every few weeks. The counsellor enjoys working with Mrs Simpson and they meet on an occasional basis for nearly two years, during which time Mrs. Simpson works through much of her grief, both about the loss of her husband and of any good relationship with her mother. She begins to adjust to life alone and is encouraged by the return of her enthusiasm to pursue long-held interests in travel, gardening and academic study.

Mrs Simpson's crisis precipitated a collapse of her rather brittle defences and the realisation that she could not continue to take care of all her emotional needs, as she had done since childhood. Her intense grief and experience of loss had generated a real need in the here-and-now for containment and support. Although she was clearly suitable for long-term psychotherapy and was in a position to afford it, her transference to the counsellor during the assessment process and to the practice as a whole as an 'environment mother' (Winnicott, 1996), who together could hold her together in 'body and soul', enabled her to ask for what she thought she needed and could manage. The counsellor realised that Mrs Simpson's capacity to ask for what she wanted marked a breakthrough in her life-long difficulty in trusting another sufficiently to ask for her needs to be met, and she was able to respond by metaphorically 'presenting the breast' when it was wanted. As Winnicott writes:

> in the early stages of the emotional development of the human infant a vital part is played by the environment which is in fact not yet separated off from the infant by the infant . . . the major changes take place in the separating-out of the mother as an objectively perceived environmental feature. If no one person is there to be mother, the infant's developmental task is, infinitely complicated . . . the environmental function involves: holding, handling and object-presenting (Winnicott, 1996, p. 111).

In this case the practice became the primitive 'environment mother' who could 'hold' and 'handle' Mrs Simpson in her distress, and the counsellor could present herself as an object/mother in a responsive way to enable a therapeutic alliance to develop.

Summary

The ongoing caseloads of counsellors working in primary care are likely to be rich and varied, provided counsellors themselves are open to using their range of skills and experience flexibly and appropriately. Inevitably, part of this work involves recognising the limits of these skills and the need to refer to others more suitably qualified. Counselling in primary care has distinctive features that are context-specific. We are not practising psychoanalysis *per se*, but as psychodynamic counsellors we are adopting an *attitude to the work* that has its roots in the pioneering research of Freud, Jung and others into the mysteries of unconscious processes. A psychodynamic understanding is likely to be a dominant and relevant principle throughout our work with patients and colleagues, as well as when thinking about practice dynamics as a whole.

The case examples in this chapter are a selection, not exhaustive, of the different styles of work with which counsellors are likely to find themselves involved. There are opportunities for working with families, where every member of the primary care team may be involved and an understanding of the psychodynamics of the situation and the projective and introjective processes at work are essential if treatment and management plans are to be in the patient's/family's best interests. Working with different ethnic groups is likely to take up a major part of counsellors' time, providing GPs are attentive enough to make appropriate referrals and counsellors courageous enough to take on this difficult work. There are opportunities for different kinds of brief therapy, for supportive counselling and for helping patients at different times with difficult life events. There are also many opportunities to purvey psychological understanding to professionals from different disciplines who work in the surgery.

The distinctive features of the work suggest a number of paradoxes: the confidence to try new things while recognising that we do not have the skills to practise all therapies; a respect for patients' right to privacy, as well as a need to communicate relevant information back to patients' referring GPs; the need for firm boundaries to create a safe container for counselling to take place but also for flexibility to accommodate the wide range of different patients who are likely to present for counselling. The management of these paradoxes is the craft of the work and will no doubt be assisted by counsellors receiving regular supervision.

Going back to Coltart's (1993, p. 18) ideas about the practice of psychotherapy, she thinks that 'dynamic psychotherapy keeps one at full stretch all the time'. Ongoing work in primary care is likely to keep most counsellors at 'full stretch' much of the time, but hopefully the learning that takes place and the rewards of the job will far outweigh the stress that goes with working at full stretch.

7

PSYCHOSOMATIC ILLNESS: THE PATH TOWARDS A COMMON LANGUAGE

The language of the body

As psychodynamic counsellors we are often accused of overvaluing, even idealising the mind and what might be called thinking, while neglecting the body and the contribution of body language and symptoms. Conversely, many GPs tend to look at symptoms in a purely physical or organic way and neglect the psychological meaning that may lie behind them. As the poet Samuel Taylor Coleridge wrote in 1796: 'I know a great many physicians, they are shallow Animals: having always employed their minds about Body and Gut, they imagine that in the whole system of things there is nothing but Gut and Body.'

The old Cartesian split between mind and body has had a detrimental effect on the entire field of mental health, including medicine and depth psychology. Conventional scientific medicine may be said to have fostered a split between the objective body and the body of subjective experience, and this has to a considerable extent permeated our own attitudes. GPs are often more comfortable treating the objective body and prescribing medicines to treat symptoms. Counsellors may become overly preoccupied with the subjective body, that is, patients' experiences or beliefs about their body, to the neglect of their actual bodily symptoms.

It is in the treatment of patients who present with psychosomatic symptoms that GPs and counsellors are likely to work most closely together, and when the members of these two professions are working in the same premises, the opportunity to engage in collaborative work and the construction of bridges across the divisive Cartesian split should be most welcome. However the opposite may happen, and it is precisely when working with patients with a psychosomatic illness that dialogue between GP and counsellor can be at its most difficult, since both may be reluctant to make the effort required to develop a common language. Counsellors working in a GP surgery are likely to meet a greater number of patients with psychosomatic symptoms than they would in their own private practices, and because of this an understanding of the meaning of symptoms is crucial.

In 1916 (p. 83) Carl Jung wrote 'There are those who neither see nor hear, but whose hands have the knack of giving expression to the contents of the unconscious.' All patients 'talk with their bodies' when they come to see us and the body may be seen to have a language of its own which is asking to be decoded and understood. In our work over the past ten years we have found it helpful to think about three different, though overlapping, forms of bodily communication from patients. These may be conscious, but are often unconscious, that is, patients may be unaware of what they are communicating and why.

First, patients' gestures, movements, ways of speaking and ways of wearing clothes may reflect their characteristic way of being. These form our impression of a patient's persona or general self-image: a woman who cannot look others in the eye; a man who always yawns before he speaks; a woman who smiles constantly.

Second, body language expresses feelings about the 'here and now' of the consultation and about the relationship between counsellor and patient. In psychodynamic language, it is about the transference, the counsellor's effect on the patient: a sudden blush, stammering and other visible anxiety symptoms such as sweating or a nervous cough are examples. These are live happenings in the room and betray areas of feeling or anxiety that reflect the nuances of what is happening at that moment and the feelings the patient may have about coming to see the counsellor.

Third, there are patients with a psychosomatic illness that may need treatment, but the illness in general, or some specific symptoms, may point to a psychological cause that needs to be understood. The first two forms of bodily communication clearly apply whenever a patient goes to see a counsellor. The third form, which concerns psychosomatic illness rather than non-verbal communication, will be the main focus of this chapter.

What is psychosomatic illness?

The formal study of psychosomatic medicine began in the 1930s, and there is now a comprehensive research and psychological literature. Traditionally the word psychosomatic has been used in a specific way to refer to actual bodily illness. Most usually it has comprised what have been called Alexander's 'holy seven' (Alexander, 1950), or the 'Chicago seven': ulcerative colitis, bronchial asthma, skin allergies, thyroid gland disease, rheumatoid arthritis, gastric ulcers and high blood pressure that has no physical determinant. The psychoanalyst Joyce McDougall (1989) has extended this list to include insomnia, migraine, accident proneness and addictions. Further additions would be eating disorders, chronic fatigue syndrome (ME) and sexual dysfunction, including impotence and frigidity.

Although sometimes used as a description of an early body–mind unity, the word psychosomatic has usually been used in a specific way to refer to actual bodily illness. As McDougall points out:

> I have come to consider as related to psychosomatic phenomena, all cases of physical damage or ill health in which psychological factors play an important role. In psychosomatic states, the body appears to be behaving in a delusional fashion, often over-functioning excessively to a degree that appears physiologically senseless. One is tempted to say that the body has gone mad (McDougall, 1989, p. 18).

Somatisation and psychosomatic illness

We all somatise at times and our bodies develop symptoms: headache, backache, whichever symptoms are our unique way of reacting to the stressful situations with which we may have to deal. On the other hand psychosomatic illness, as described in this chapter, may be observed as a familiar, frequent, often intractable response to particular situations when an actual illness develops. A patient who consults the doctor about stomach pains following the death of his father from stomach cancer, or a patient who complains of 'a pain in the neck' after a huge row with her husband, are somatising reactively. This is different from a patient who repeatedly presents in the surgery with respiratory tract infections, panic attacks or a series of different physical symptoms.

A psychodynamic understanding of psychosomatic illness

McDougall (ibid., p. 28). believes that psychosomatic patients are suffering from deprivations that began very early in life:

> certain allergic, gastric, cardiac and other reactions may be a somatic expression of an attempt to protect oneself against truly archaic, libidinal and narcissistic longings that are felt to be life-endangering, much as a small infant might experience the threat of death.

When this happens, she believes that the psyche warns the body of danger and bypasses the use of language so that whatever is threatening cannot be thought about and hence is somatised. These profound splits between psyche and soma occur when 'separation and difference are feared as experiences that may destroy the sense of self' (ibid., p. 42). Coltart (1992, p. 13) would agree with McDougall in locating the roots of psychosomatic disturbance in early infancy: 'If I were to condense into one sentence what the hidden central dynamic was, I would say it was pre-verbal, never thinkable, never expressible rage with the mother, rooted in a period before attainment of the depressive position'.

Whilst these psychoanalysts seem to agree that psychosomatic symptoms have their roots in the earliest phases of life, why some patients develop psychosomatic rather than other symptoms remains a mystery. One hypothesis may be that many psychosomatic patients are suffering from particular disturbances in what are called 'vitality affects', emanating from the time when sensuous communication between mother and baby can critically affect emotional development (Wiener, 1994). Stern (1985) uses the term vitality affects to describe a quality of experience that constitutes an important aspect of intersubjective relating. He makes a distinction between what may be called 'category affects' such as anger, sadness, joy, fear or disgust, and vitality affects, which cannot be classified in terms of these readily recognisable emotions as they do not have names and will be highly individual. Zinkin (1991) sees vitality affects as 'the patient's particular form of being alive', which he likens to musical signs (crescendo, allegro ma non troppo and so on), rather than the actual notes to be played. The mother, in trying to tune into her baby: 'gives meaning to what the baby expresses and is concerned, at the same time, with the *regulation of affects* and levels of arousal and the transition between them as well as the satisfaction of basic bodily needs' (ibid., p. 53).

Although other authors do not necessarily choose to use the term vitality affects, there seems to be a growing body of evidence in contemporary psychoanalytic literature to support the view that such disturbances can have a major detrimental effect in later life. For the baby, the mother's face, voice, skin and smell may be as important as, if not more important than, the physical breast and experiences connected with sucking. The breast may have become overdetermined. The liveliness and sensitivity with which a mother tunes into her baby's communications in a bodily way constitutes an essential element in the journey towards symbolisation.

McDougall's case illustrations of psychosomatic patients suggest similar conclusions. A number of her patients show 'the effects [psychosomatic illness] in adulthood of a pre-verbal child's early perception of affectless modes of functioning as a way of combating psychological pain, early frustration and panic' (McDougall, 1989, p. 6).

In his book *The Skin Ego*, Anzieu (1989, p. 39) puts it cogently: 'the infant experiences maternal gestures first as a sensory stimulus, then as a communication. The massage becomes a message'. McDougall quotes Henry Maudsley, London's famous nineteenth-century anatomist: 'the sorrow that has no vent in tears makes other organs weep' (McDougall, 1989 p. 139). Patients suffering from psychosomatic illness are weeping or perhaps raging with their bodies about a very early disturbance that cannot as yet be put into words, thought about or dreamed about.

Psychosomatic illness and hysteria

When assessing patients who arrive at the practice with severe physical symptoms, it may be difficult to make a distinction between those symptoms that are psychosomatic and those which may be more helpfully thought of as hysterical. It was of course Freud (1923) who said that 'the ego is first and foremost a bodily ego', and it was the presentation of hysterical symptoms that led to the birth of our profession. Freud (1895) believed that when a hysterical patient does not know something, he or she actually does not *want* to know it. He suggested that the reason for this denial lies in repressed phantasies of early sexual seduction that find somatic rather than psychic expression. Freud's view of the common hysterical structure that underlies all clinical presentations is expressed in the following quotation:

the specificity of hysteria is to be found in the prevalence of a certain kind of identification and of certain mechanisms (particularly repression, which is often explicit) in an emergence of the Oedipal conflict occurring mainly in the phallic and oral libidinal spheres (Laplanche and Pontalis, 1980, p. 195).

The two important points here are (1) the content of what is split off and repressed in hysteria is likely to be sexual, and (2) that it will centre on problems of 'triangulation', that is, on the difficulty of managing the Oedipal rather than the pre-Oedipal situation.

Bollas' more contemporary views on hysteria helpfully supplement our knowledge:

> few patients enjoy the possession of an analyst quite like the hysteric . . . such people seem almost wholly concerned to grip the analyst in order to create an unforgettable vision, and such an aim takes precedence over thinking, reflecting and understanding (Bollas, 1987, p. 190).

He believes that hysterical conversion still exists, but that it is now often the therapist who *'suffers the effects of hysterical conversion'* through general paralysis, rather than its appearance directly as a bodily symptom in the patient. His idea must surely emerge out of recent conceptualisations about countertransference and projective identification.

Khan (1983, p. 52) believes that hysteria finds character and shape in adolescence and that 'the hysteric in early childhood deals with the failures of good-enough mothering and care by precocious sexual development . . . in lieu of affective relating and ego-functions'.

There has been recent debate about the usefulness of the term hysteria (Brenman, 1985; Bell, 1992), and it has undoubtedly acquired a meaning that seems derogatory, particularly to women. It is true that patients today rarely present with full conversion hysteria, that is, limbs that have become paralysed, and the term no longer seems relevant to contemporary psychopathology. However counsellors still come across patients in the surgery who may be described as having hysterical symptoms. The reader will probably recognise these patients, who present in a theatrical or dramatic fashion, often exaggerating many of their symptoms in an overpowering way that makes it difficult to think clearly about them. It is understandable that they turn first of all to the GP practice, precisely because the distinction between hysterical and psychosomatic symptoms is often difficult to make, both by the patients and the professionals. The GP is likely to be the first port of call to assess the nature of (organic) symptoms. In contrast to psychosomatic illness, which generally implies some very early damage, hysterical symptoms are usually not life-threatening, either physiologically or psychologically.

Psychosomatic illness in primary care

A key question is, which of the many patients with psychosomatic symptoms will the GP choose to refer to the counsellor working in the practice? The challenging opportunities for GPs and counsellors to collaborate productively when working with psychosomatic patients have already been emphasised, and to a large extent successful collaboration depends on the effect the patient has on the GP. Some GPs prefer to treat symptoms organically and are reluctant, as mentioned in earlier chapters, to open what might turn out to be a Pandora's Box if they start to ask questions to discover the meaning of the symptoms. Other GPs find it difficult to know the right questions to ask. Furthermore many of the patients who present to the GP with psychosomatic symptoms are not remotely interested in understanding the causes of their symptoms. They simply want the GP to 'make them better', to 'do something'. These are the kinds of patient who are likely to visit the GP's consulting room frequently, asking for a series of referrals to different specialists in the hope that someone will find 'the magic touch' to make them better.

CASE EXAMPLE: RENATE

Over a period of two months Renate visits her GP with a number of minor physical complaints – a sore throat, split nails, thrush, a rash on her back, to name but a few. The GP takes each complaint seriously and recommends relevant treatment in a friendly and helpful way. Renate is an extremely attractive beauty consultant who has recently come from abroad to live in England. It does not occur to the GP that these minor ailments are connected and that something else is worrying her that she can not talk about, but which could account for her repeated visits to see him. Eventually, Renate asks if she may see the practice counsellor. It emerges that her symptoms are masking her depression about the difficulty of adjusting to life in a new country, and more important they are masking her guilt about becoming involved with a man in London, even though she has a regular boyfriend in her country of origin.

For this GP, asking relevant questions about the patient's emotional life in order to discover whether there was anything significant behind her physical symptoms was daunting. A later discussion between the counsellor and the GP revealed that the GP found this woman very attractive. Concentrating on her physical problems alone helped him keep a safe distance between them. The GP was unconsciously defending himself against an erotic transference to his patient, which might be awakened if he encouraged her to talk freely about emotions that were bothering her and were probably related to her physical symptoms.

Many patients with psychosomatic symptoms require both medical and psychological support. While patients may have a strong preference for one particular approach, it is most important for the GP to be tuned in to the possible psychological meanings behind the patient's presentation. On the other hand, if the psychosomatic symptoms are life-threatening, for example asthma or respiratory illnesses, the counsellor will need to remain in touch with the patient's current state of physical health if any psychological treatment is offered.

Who is treatable?

Only some patients suffering from psychosomatic complaints are suitable for counselling, and a major task for the counsellor presented with such patients is accurately to assess which patients to work with. Patients with psychosomatic symptoms who seek private counselling have already made a personal choice and are motivated to participate in counselling. Usually they are taken on. In primary care the situation is likely to be more complex. A considerable number of patients with psychosomatic symptoms never choose to see a counsellor. In some cases this may be because they prefer a hands-on approach and are drawn towards alternative therapies such as massage, acupuncture, osteopathy or homeopathy. Other patients, as already mentioned, are insufficiently interested in the nature of their symptoms to undertake what can sometimes be a lengthy and painful period of counselling. Some would like counselling but are actually unsuitable.

Suitable patients

Some somatic symptoms, if caught early, can be most helpfully treated in the practice before they become chronic. The presence of a counsellor in the practice represents a window of opportunity as patients usually go to their GP when their symptom is causing them the most anxiety. Rather than volunteer for counselling, some of these patients may be 'sent' by the GP, but once they begin to talk, some psychological connections may be made and progress is possible.

CASE EXAMPLE: BELINDA

Belinda, a woman in her early thirties, complains to her GP about persistent headaches and neck pain. She is a small, rather overweight woman who looks depressed. The GP asks if there is anything worrying her at the moment and Belinda tells her that she is very jealous of the relationship between her new baby and her husband. The GP asks her if she would like to see the practice counsellor and she agrees. It emerges that Belinda had two miscarriages before the birth of her baby, neither of which she mourned. She comes from a family of five children where the mother is extremely competent and elegant and managed to bring up all the children, hold down a full-time job and continue to look attractive. The patient feels envious of her mother as she has only managed to work part time and is wobbly about her sense of herself as a woman. These long-standing problems with her mother were reawakened when her baby was born. The doctor is not afraid to ask questions and is quick to pick up the emotions behind the symptoms. She realises that referral to the counsellor is an appropriate next step. The counsellor sees Belinda on her own, then invites her to bring her husband to the second session. They both find the opportunity to talk about their relationship very helpful, and Belinda's husband, who is most supportive, helps his wife to see that their child actually has a very strong attachment to its mother. They agree to have six sessions of joint work with the counsellor, after which Belinda might consider some individual therapy for herself to work on issues specific to her, including her relationship with her mother.

In this example the doctor was sufficiently interested in her patient's life and prepared to ask relevant questions in order to discover whether her physical symptoms were a way of unconsciously trying to get help for deeper, psychological matters. The GP was psychologically minded and able to pick up the underlying meaning of her patient's symptoms, to work with them for a while so that she could facilitate what turned out to be a helpful referral to the counsellor working in the practice.

CASE EXAMPLE: KEVIN

Thirty year old Kevin comes to see his family doctor about a sudden and severe attack of psoriasis. He is stressed at work and the GP recommends that he takes three months sick leave, as well as giving him a number of remedies for his skin problem. He returns to the GP after two and a half months complaining that the psoriasis is no better. The doctor then decides to refer him to the practice counsellor. He is reluctant to converse with the counsellor and seems to feel more comfortable with the idea that his symptoms have a physical rather than a psychological cause. It is evident that he feels stigmatised and threatened by the idea that his body is reacting to what could be an emotional problem. The reason for this emerges during three meetings with him.

He is the eldest of three children. He is close to his mother, who has a history of depressive illness, for which she has had some counselling, but he feels distant from his father, with whom he finds it extremely difficult to communicate. He feels he is carrying the burden of having to be the successful one in the family. He is the only child to have gone to university and is now in a well-paid though demanding job as a stockbroker in a large firm in central London. It gradually emerges that two events occurred just before his skin condition erupted. After many years of secrecy he had finally told his mother that he was gay. Although on the surface she seemed to respond in a very loving and accepting way, a few weeks later she made a suicide attempt.

The young man had failed to connect his itchy and painful skin with these two significant events, because the connection was too painful and his body was behaving in a 'delusional' fashion to protect him from emotional pain and some conscious understanding of it. To accept the psychological meaning of his psoriasis would place him dangerously close to his mother, who was very fragile psychologically and, as he saw it, counselling had made little difference to her depression. However he came to see that although he needed to take seriously the messages coming from his body, they did not necessarily mean that he was going to become as ill as his mother. He agreed to accept a referral for private psychotherapy so that he could talk in depth about the aspects of his early life that were intruding into the present in this distressing way. In this case example, sensibly the GP first tried to treat the patient's symptoms medically. When this failed to make any difference, referral to the counsellor was the obvious and helpful next step.

All three of the patients described in the case examples above (Renate, Belinda and Kevin) had relatively mild physical symptoms that appeared to be caused by the psychological effects of a particular situation. However patients with more chronic psychosomatic illness should not necessarily be excluded from the possibility of psychological help. Some patients with massively thick medical files can be well-supported by the practice counsellor. The nature of the work in the first instance may involve drawing the GP towards the idea that making yet another referral to an outside specialist is not necessarily in the patient's best interests. The significance of helping chronic patients successfully to manage to contain their symptoms should not be underemphasised. However such patients are often extremely demanding and taxing for the GP, and some supportive sessions with the counsellor can be most helpful for patients as a way of allowing the GP a well-earned breathing space.

Elderly patients are frequently anxious about somatic symptoms, indeed some may turn out to be serious or even life-threatening. While some older patients have a history of psychosomatic illness, others come to the counsellor from the GP with a particular agenda – the wish is for the counsellor to be reassuring and to convey that there is nothing to worry about. Sometimes, after discussions with the GP, this is possible. On other occasions, however, careful work is needed to help elderly patients come to terms with real, irritating symptoms, and with diminishing physical resources. Some patients benefit from a supportive, encouraging, positive approach to make the most of their lives and to try to come to terms with often crippling anxieties. On other occasions a more analytic, in-depth approach is suitable and usable and can be most productive.

Unsuitable patients

Finally, what of the patients who are unsuitable for counselling? It is important to understand what makes someone unsuitable, and as Joyce McDougall (1989, p. 8) aptly puts it, 'psychosomatic symptoms are an attempt at self-cure'. For all patients, psychosomatic symptoms are a way of dealing with some inexpressible pain or grief, and in some cases this can be of psychotic proportions. The symptoms may be easier to bear than the risk of opening up the painful issues that lie behind them. With a skilled counsellor, and the possibility of more frequent treatment sessions than is usually possible in primary care, such patients may get in touch with some of their anxieties, which may then be contained and understood during course of counselling. For others there is a risk of breakdown or psychosis, and caution about treatment recommendations is likely to be necessary.

CASE EXAMPLE: FATIMA

Thirty nine year old Fatima is referred to the counsellor by her GP. She fails to attend her first three appointments, but much to the surprise of the counsellor she arrives at the fourth. She presents as extremely depressed and is taking quite a high dose of antidepressants. She wants to sleep all day, cannot work and has recently begun to experience intense muscle spasms. Her mother died six months previously in a 'surgical accident' and she is devastated by the loss and dreams about her mother almost every night. Her father too was killed ten years ago in a car accident that occurred when her brother-in-law was driving. Her brother-in-law was unhurt and she is deeply angry with him for surviving and seeming not to care about what happened. She is also furious with the surgeon who 'killed' her mother. She talks continuously about her symptoms. Any intervention from the counsellor that tries to link her symptoms to these two traumatic events is met with a catalogue of further physical symptoms, as if the counsellor is not hearing what she is saying. There is no window of psychological opportunity to begin a conversation and her body is all that is available for discussion. She does not possess the language to talk about herself psychologically, and rather despondently the counsellor refers her back to the GP.

This patient could be said to be unsuitable for counselling for the following reasons (McDougall, 1989):

- She showed no motivation to seek psychological help.
- She showed little awareness of the psychic suffering/mental pain behind her symptoms.
- There was no interest in a search for self-knowledge, rather a wish to continue to blame others and obtain her revenge by identifying herself as 'just an ill person'.
- It was doubtful whether the psychological pain that counselling would open up would be bearable.
- She appeared to have no real ability to receive help – nothing was right or good enough

In our experience it can be complicated to counsel patients from some ethnic groups who present with psychosomatic illness, and it is often these patients who are most likely to miss or cancel their appointments. In many cultures, particularly Eastern, Middle-Eastern and some Afro-Caribbean cultures, counselling is viewed with suspicion and indeed is seen to be a weakness that is likely to gain the disapproval of relatives, friends and peers. Medical and hands-on physical treatments are much more acceptable. Counsellors working with such patients may have no special training in this area and will need to understand these difficulties, be aware of their own prejudices and be flexible in their approach if the patient is to remain engaged with the process.

Locke outlines a number of helpful principles of multicultural practice that counsellors in primary care would do well to bear in mind. He stresses the importance of cultural group membership:

> the cultural group serves as the basis for individuals to become humanised. Each individual becomes fully human through the process of participating in a cultural group or groups. . . . Each individual is seeking a personal identity by acknowledging an identity with a cultural group while living in a world community (Locke, 1989, p. xiii).

He encourages us to remember that styles of counselling and education are not value-free and that we need to remain vigilant about the systemic dimensions of racism and alienation, which may become areas of countertransference difficulty for the counsellor: 'multiculturalism is not simply the addition of content about ethnically diverse peoples; it involves rethinking the policies related to the use of all material in a (educational) curriculum' (ibid., p. 159). Practices frequently have access to interpreters to facilitate a dialogue. Similarly, specialist counselling services for ethnic minority groups have mushroomed over recent years (see the list of useful organisations in Appendix B), and there are often local resources that GPs and counsellors can use creatively.

Ways of working together

The development of productive working relationships requires time, energy, some space and capacity for reflection. For professionals who come from different training backgrounds and have different cultural traditions this is not without its hazards. In order to work together successfully with psychosomatic patients, both GPs and counsellors need to be comfortable in their roles and know the limits of those roles. Patients with a 'fat' medical file and an extensive history of psychosomatic illness are likely to visit their GP frequently. Some GPs may narcissistically need patients to depend on them, others may be uncomfortable with too much dependence.

The way in which the referral to the counsellor is made is crucial. Whilst not all GPs are particularly interested in the psychological side of medicine, it is desirable that they develop some skill at asking the 'right' questions to help facilitate a referral to the counsellor (see Chapter 4 on referrals). At the same time it must be remembered that GPs have overall responsibility for their patients, and this is particularly important for patients with what can be life-threatening psychosomatic symptoms that need medical treatment. If patient and counsellor decide on a psychological treatment, it is essential for the GP to be kept informed of what is going on and adequate avenues of communication between GP and counsellor should be kept open at all times. On the whole, counsellors have a broader repertoire of tools and responses than GPs with which to explore the meaning of psychosomatic symptoms. They are more accustomed to understanding the nature of defences, their rigidity and what lies behind them. Similarly the counsellor, if well-trained, will have a broader range of suitable treatment options, including working with 'psychosomatic families', where it is necessary to understand the meaning of one individual's symptoms as part of a wider family problem.

Summary

This chapter has illustrated how working with psychosomatic patients inevitably throws GP and counsellor together into some kind of alliance. Whether or not this alliance turns out to be fruitful depends ultimately on the willingness of both to remain open-minded to the views of the other, so that the necessary joint management plans can be made. The case examples used in this chapter illustrate how GPs need to be psychologically sensitive to the emotional components of physical symptoms. This is critical when trying to decide which patients could benefit from a referral to the counsellor and which are likely to be more helpfully contained by the GP and a more medical approach. Consultations with the counsellor to discuss patients who present with psychosomatic illness not only benefit the patients they discuss, but also provide an opportunity for the GP and counsellor to try to understand each other better and learn a common language.

The case examples also illustrate the power of unconscious forces and how they can influence both doctor and patient in their understanding of symptoms and how to treat them. In the example of Kevin, who was suffering from severe psoriasis, with the help of the doctor and the counsellor the patient gradually began to realise that he needed psychological treatment in conjunction with medical help to alleviate his symptoms. It seemed likely that his symptoms were linked to two significant and difficult events in his life, and that he was defending himself against painful links with his mother and the fear of becoming like her. For Renate, the somatising woman who had recently come from abroad to live in England, the doctor's attraction to his patient was unconsciously limiting his capacity to think sufficiently broadly about treatment options. In the words of Tom Main, a well-known British psychoanalyst:

> the use of treatments in the service of the therapist's unconscious is often superbly creative . . . there can never be certain guarantee that the therapist facing great and resistant distress will be immune from using interpretations in the way in which nurses use sedatives . . . to soothe themselves when desperate, and to escape from their own distressing ailment of ambivalence and hatred. (Main, 1989a, p. 14)

In a profession that requires accurate diagnoses and quick decisions, it is difficult for doctors to create the space and time to think about patients, to tolerate not knowing, and to bear the powerful forces that can affect the doctor–patient relationship. In a lecture on the medical defences that doctors use against involvement with their patients, Main (1989b, p. 205) compares the experiences of a soldier fighting in the war with those of a doctor. He observed that fighting spirit and the will to win were at their lowest among those troops in actual combat/contact with the enemy: 'fighting morale seemed to rise with the square of the distance from the enemy until, well behind the armies, at the Army Group Rear Headquarters, it reached its zenith'. GPs are in the medical front line, and like soldiers they may at times have to contain high levels of inner and outer stress, which can only be made endurable by finding ways of protecting themselves. Main describes these defences as 'attitudinal, social, geographic, or temporal changes and manoeuvres that, no matter how common or medically hallowed, can be seen to have been devised primarily out of the doctor's need to diminish his anxiety rather than primarily for the patient's welfare' (ibid., p. 206).

Counsellors too may become caught up with institutional defences against anxiety. It is most likely that these processes will be observable in their work with psychosomatic patients, so often the most taxing of patients for the GP and the counsellor, and so often the patients who unknowingly throw GPs and counsellors into close proximity with each other. However it is this 'throwing together' that leads to productive and exciting alliances and creative treatments for the patient.

8

KEY PROFESSIONAL ISSUES

The changing professional culture of primary care

A wind of change is sweeping through the health service and its repercussions are being felt at the grass-roots level in primary care. Inevitably this is affecting patient care. Doctors' and counsellors' expectations, their roles and their relationships are being redefined. Patients are now expected to be more responsible for their own health. Exercise, diet and a healthy lifestyle are a few examples of this. Old assumptions about universal care 'from cradle to grave' are changing, and now that the dependency culture of the postwar decades is being swept aside, governments are urging us to invest in pensions to see us through our old age. The same applies to primary care and the rise of fund-holding practices. Doctors have had to reassess their allocation of funds. Who gets what and how much has been delegated to the local level, which means that decision making in health care is community- and patient-responsive. Choice has been the political justification for many of the changes, but few believe that there has been an equitable distribution of resources geographically and generationally, and even across gender and illness lines. While fund-holding practices have broken new ground by providing on-site counselling services for their patients, this may be financially motivated: counselling is cheaper than psychiatry. There are cases where counselling is beneficial, provided it is underpinned by adequate resources and is part of a larger network of caring that can be called on to assist with troublesome cases. There is evidence to suggest that this is not happening. Without recourse to broader networks, including health visitors, social workers and psychotherapists, counselling in primary care cannot succeed.

Interprofessional relationships

The changes referred to above highlight the need for healthcare professionals to cooperate with one another in the interests of improved patient care. Relationships with other professional groups have been a running theme of the BMA's ethical guidance. The BMA recognises other professional groups once they have acquired statutory status and relies on their codes of ethics to govern professional behaviour and maintain high standards of practice. The GMC (1993, p. 17) has consistently welcomed 'the growing contributions made to healthcare by persons who have been trained to perform specialised functions'. Doctors recognise that other disciplines can offer their skills independently, outside their sphere of responsibility, so that independent professionals assume responsibility for their own actions.

In recent decades there has been a shift in healthcare policy away from institutions towards the community, where emphasis is placed on a multidisciplinary approach to health management. Medicine has also witnessed a decline in its traditional monopoly on health matters in favour of interdisciplinary or team approaches, and a consumer-led interest in the potential of other therapies. The independence of other health professionals has become increasingly recognised and respected. This movement takes us into an arena where key professional dilemmas for GPs and counsellors will become apparent.

Liaison with other disciplines

It is estimated that about 65 per cent of UK patients use non-conventional methods of treatment as a supplement to orthodox medicine (Thomas *et al.*, 1991). Many doctors employ professionals from other disciplines and GPs have been encouraged to do this since 1990 by government-led contractual changes. The GMC (1993, paras 42–3) makes it clear that 'a doctor who delegates treatment or other procedures must be satisfied that the person to whom they are delegating is competent to carry them out'.

For professionals who are accountable to a recognised registering and disciplinary body, this poses few problems. The British Association of Counselling (BAC) is the professional umbrella association for most counsellors. The BAC sets the standards for counselling training, and can be consulted when a doctor seeks to validate a counsellor's credentials. The Counselling in General Practice Working Party of the Royal College of General Practitioners (RCGP) adopted the use of the term 'counselling' to refer to trained counsellors undertaking counselling as defined by the BAC, with its distinctive ethic and philosophy, and specifically referred to the patients' capacity for self-determination:

> Counselling is the skilled and principled use of relationships which develop self-knowledge, emotional acceptance and growth, and personal resources. The overall aim is to live more fully and satisfyingly. Counselling may be concerned with addressing and resolving specific problems, making decisions, coping with crises, working through feelings and inner-conflict, or improving relationships with others. The counsellor's role is to facilitate the client's work in ways that respect the client's values, personal resources, and capacity for self-determination (quoted in Bond, 1995, p. 5).

The growing inclination to supplement orthodox medicine, together with the burden of fund management, have forced GPs to rely on ancillary disciplines to ease their load. Delayed feedback, longer lines of communication and the freer availability of restricted information can all strain the boundaries of confidentiality. This leads us to a key professional issue.

Confidentiality

Confidentiality is a traditional professional principle and a practical requirement shared by doctors, counsellors and their patients.

Privacy

Privacy is a fundamental right that allows individuals to decide the manner and extent to which information about themselves is shared with others. Self-determination in this respect is also central to preservation of the dignity and integrity of the individual. According to the BMA (1993), on occasion public interest may override the primacy of individual privacy, but in such instances the facts must be examined closely to determine whether there is a genuine necessity for disclosure.

Secrecy

Confidentiality is not the same as secrecy. Confusion between the two terms arises when patients expect all revelations within the doctor's surgery to remain veiled in secrecy. There are however many occasions when doctors believe it necessary to make the contents of such conversations available to others. Although this is not the secrecy the patient may have sought, the doctor's actions remain within the bounds of confidentiality; external and internal referrals, statutory requirements to report notifiable diseases and certain criminal activities must be reported by law.

The ethos of confidentiality

Long before the contemporary emphasis on privacy, the principle of confidentiality was germane to the ethics of medical practice. It is also an overriding professional principle in psychotherapy and counselling. The function of the confidentiality principle is to protect the doctor–patient and counsellor–patient relationship, although at the present time neither doctors nor counsellors are shielded by legal privilege, unlike communications between lawyers and their clients. The concept goes back to the time of Hippocrates and is restated in the International Code of Medical Ethics, which says that 'a doctor must preserve absolute confidentiality on all he knows about his patient, even after the patient's death'.

However issues of confidentiality are beset with contradictions. Professional bodies recognise that new pressures, largely outside the control of the professionals, are being brought to bear on the confidentiality rule. These come from changing patterns of health care delivery, the increasing emphasis on health care promotion and preventive measures, and the commercial demand for health-related information. Many find it hard to believe that apparently small compromises in confidentiality, made in the name of efficiency or convenience, erode patients' rights.

Information has always been given to doctors and counsellors with the intention of providing a sound basis for appropriate care. Increasingly, details about life-style and family history are being sought as part of health promotion and research, but personal, health and family data can also be used for a wide range of other purposes, such as insurance policies, housing applications or referrals to specialists. Health records have an increasingly important social function and doctors and counsellors frequently complain that, instead of preserving the secrecy of medical, personal and family data, they expend much effort on circulating it to different recipients who sometimes share ill-defined obligations regarding its confidentiality.

Sharing information

Doctors and counsellors have a duty to preserve the bounds of confidentiality. To reveal information there must be adequate grounds, and it usually requires the patient's consent. One criterion governing confidential disclosures is that the receiving health professional has a demonstrable 'need to know' that particular piece of information in the interests of patient care. Increasingly care is provided by multidisciplinary teams and agencies collaborating with each other in difficult cases, such as those where the welfare of children is at stake, and it is important that patients are aware of this and explicitly agree to information being passed on to those who need to know. Passing on information cannot be justified for any other reason. The right to privacy is considered an essential element of human rights, but it is not absolute.

Models of confidentiality

Confidentiality is fundamental to both doctors and counsellors individually and as partners in a multidisciplinary team. In such a new and uncertain environment, counsellors seem to rely on one of two broad models:

- Some believe that all exchanges between patient and counsellor are absolutely confidential and that GPs need know nothing about them.
- Some believe that as members of a multidisciplinary team, joint confidentiality applies to the team as a whole.

The second model acknowledges that it is in the patient's best interest to pool some knowledge among appropriate members of the team, particularly the GP, so that information is shared on a 'need-to-know' basis. This approach is a pragmatic one from the standpoint of counsellors as they acquire a great deal of background information that the GP does not need in the general management of patient care. It is rare for GPs to need more than basic information about patients' counselling sessions. Most of the subtleties of the counselling session are of interest only to the counsellor and the patient.

Staff meetings

Confidentiality in primary care has more than one dimension. There are times when conversations about patients are held in order to help members of the team increase their psychological understanding of patients generally. For these conversations to be effective, there needs to be a 'space for thinking', a protected time for staff members to meet. These meetings, like counselling sessions, have a defined membership, start and end punctually and should not be interrupted. Telephones should not be answered and the doors should be kept closed with the 'engaged' sign on. These meetings have a clear purpose and everyone bears responsibility for ensuring that the professional nature of the discussions is maintained. The counselling model of paying attention to the details of time, space and boundaries can serve as a model for responsible interdisciplinary work for the members of the primary care team. Boundaries are often lax. Staff may talk about patients aloud and patient information may be visible from the reception area. The message should be clear: privacy and respect for the patient have been thought about and implemented. The meetings should be conducted confidentially and professionally in the interests of mutual learning. When meeting with professional colleagues, the principles of confidentiality may have to be adapted, but the core element of respect for the patient must never be lost.

Whether counsellors are working directly with patients or meeting with colleagues to discuss their patients, or even communicating with outside agencies about patients, say in preparing a referral, any information that needs to be passed on must be handled sensitively and with the patient's consent.

Written notes and use of computers

Confidentiality in counselling cannot be addressed without stating what should be put into the medical notes. There are cases where note-taking is an extremely delicate issue when dealing with health centre staff. In such cases, notes may not be taken at all. This issue is complicated by the widespread use of computers, which allow quick and easy retrieval of information by a whole variety of personnel who have access to the health centre's computer system. While computers allow urgent information to be communicated quickly, technology has increased the danger of patient information falling into the wrong hands. Some counsellors prefer to store their notes at home, perhaps hoping to ensure greater confidentiality that way, but they should be aware that the Data Protection Act applies to them too, and even privately held notes can be subpoenaed. Patients' statutory right to access to their own records also needs to be considered as this is bound to influence the kind of information counsellors record.

Whether counsellors keep handwritten notes or use computers, many compile brief 'thumb-nail' summaries of interviews for their records. Counsellors may want to keep separate detailed notes on those patients they discuss with their supervisors. One of our colleagues offered us the following piece of sensible guidance on note-taking: 'they should contain only what you would not mind appending to the tree on the village green'. Patients are anxious about the safety of having their personal details stored in a computer. Computers offer built-in protection in the form of pass-words and other security arrangements, but even with the most sophisticated safeguards, counsellors should be cautious and reassure themselves that all aspects of confidentiality are being observed.

The new recording methods employed in primary care have implications for everyone. Computerisation is here to stay, and if used wisely it can bring enormous benefits. It is easy to claim that 'security breaches never happen here', or to take the view that occasional lapses are the price to be paid for a streamlined system and improved efficiency. Patients' feelings and fantasies surrounding the location of their notes and how they are handled should be respected and every safeguard employed. We should bear in mind that communications flow around the practice setting fairly freely:

- When patients arrive for their appointments, their medical folders are stacked on the receptionist's counter, to be collected by the doctor when he or she calls the patient from the waiting room. These folders and their contents can sometimes be seen by other patients.
- Professional staff may loiter in the reception area and discuss their patients aloud.
- Active computer screens may still display information about a previous patient.

Funding psychological services

Since its inception in 1948, the pride of the British NHS has been that medical services are free at the point of delivery. The patient does not pay for treatment and health care professionals expect to be able to deliver the best care possible within the constraints of supply and demand. However over the years, public expectations of doctors and health care services have risen sharply. Doctors are rushed off their feet, waiting rooms are rife with stress, confusion and unhappiness. The faster the patient load is mopped up, the faster the waiting rooms refill, so that GP stress is continuously compounded. Are the problems they see medical *or* social? Or medical *and* social?

Clearly a significant proportion of cases presenting in primary care are not strictly medical and are not treatable by traditional medical methods. In response GPs have begun to introduce a whole range of ancillary services. These may include visits by hospital consultants with various specialities, or other services such as a practice nurse, a baby clinic, well-women and well-men clinics, homeopathy, chiropody, osteopathy, physiotherapy, dietetics, counselling and so on. The result of local arrangements of this breadth is that the patient load of doctors is reduced but they remain at the hub of their patients' treatment plans and retain overall control of their patients' care.

Patients presenting with psychological problems in a primary care setting can be attended to quickly and cheaply. GPs assess their patients' overall medical, social, family and psychological condition and decide which problems are within the competence of the psychological specialists on hand. It is said that 80 per cent of doctors' time is taken up by 20 per cent of patients whose needs may not be purely medical. Many of these people are drawn to their doctors for reasons of dependency, loneliness, fear, isolation or apathy, and although they may not overtly reveal the underlying problem, it can be recognised and brought to the attention of a counsellor, who may be able to shed light on the patients' use of illnesses to communicate inner psychological needs.

In the last five years, however, government funding to set up specialist clinics has been reduced, because the health authorities consider that some services are not strictly medical, but rather expensive ways of ridding GPs of their neurotic and demanding patients. The result has been a more disciplined consideration of referrals to all ancillary services in the practice, including counselling. Critical studies have been undertaken recently to assess the contribution counsellors have made to patient health (see Chapter 9 on research). As a consequence of this research, counselling has had to redefine itself more precisely and make a case for itself as a vital adjunct to medical services in the relief of pain, stress and a variety of physical symptoms. Psychological needs alone are no longer considered sufficiently pressing to justify the allocation of resources. Grants for new specialist clinics within primary care are drying up. After a decade of expanding services, we can now expect that some will be withdrawn or centralised once more. Many GPs now protest that it is impossible to cover everything, and given the choice they would prefer to attend to problems that are strictly medical. Others insist on having a counselling service in their surgeries, validating their commitment to a holistic approach to patient care. The fragile political and economic climate means that the future of counselling in primary care is a key professional issue and may depend on its ability to demonstrate its worth.

Communication

Current changes in primary care demand wide consultation and communication between professions at both national and local level. Although research has highlighted the need for counselling to hone its methods and increase its effectiveness, GPs seem satisfied with the status quo, especially where 'heart-sink' patients are concerned. The following example shows what can be achieved by sensitive and honest discussion about a difficult case. Here communication facilitated a radical shift in established patterns of relating to difficult patients.

CASE EXAMPLE: THE DYNAMICS OF PRACTICE MEETINGS

At a practice meeting attended by two GP partners, a trainee GP and three counsellors, a GP and the trainee agree to present one of their 'heart-sink' cases for discussion – two children aged five and seven who have presented with their parents at the surgery on numerous occasions with dyslexia, compounded by a range of behavioural problems such as uncontrollable temper tantrums, excessive clinging to the mother, battering and stabbing each other. Strangely the children are regarded as well-behaved at school and get on with their work. The father has been seen once by the counsellor, to whom he spoke about the difficulty of controlling his two children. He said his wife had left the family on several occasions, giving no indication of when she might return, if at all. During these absences, she stayed with her mother, who suffers from Huntington's Chorea and dementia. The trainee GP explains to the meeting that Huntington's Chorea is a genetic disease: females have a 50 per cent chance of developing the disease if their mothers have had it. The onset occurs in middle age, and once it establishes itself the victim dies within two to three years. There is no medical cure. The view amongst the GPs is that Huntington's Chorea and its associated dementia are difficult and intractable and best 'exported' from the surgery as soon as possible.

An awkward silence follows and one of the counsellors then suggests that a review of models of work might be necessary and that the counsellors in the practice might contribute to this review. Current models of work seem to be based on the principle of extrusion rather than containment, especially in the case of patients whose problems do not fit neat medical categories. One GP partner is excited by the possibility of extending medical care by developing new ways of looking at patients. Much to everyone's surprise, this GP says that her association with the counsellors in the practice over the previous six years has radically altered her way of thinking about medicine: 'life has never been the same since the counsellor discussed case X with me'. She recalls that during the early years of her medical practice she had been fired with enthusiasm to treat and cure patients. Seven years later she had become disillusioned and pessimistic with many of the medical aspects of her practice, but over the last few years she has recovered her sense of mission, acquired greater wisdom and patience and realises that patients will not always recover their health as a result of her interventions.

The meeting discusses the idea of containment and the important role it can play in primary care, since patients such as the family described will always return to the surgery. It is noted that the family has not kept its appointments at the family therapy clinic. Parallels are drawn with other 'heartsink' families, for whom strenuous efforts have been made to obtain specialist help, all of which have come to nothing because the families have sabotaged the arrangements. The patients appear to be saying that they perceive the surgery as their main source of help, and they want their doctors to be available to talk to them about incurable, life-threatening problems.

All present are buoyed up by this meeting and agree to have regular discussions about individual patients and families, as well as to address a variety of other specific problems such as alcoholism among women patients, of whom the practice has a large number.

This staff meeting felt like a turning point in the life of the practice. It provided an opportunity for the team to discuss a difficult problem. Attitudes towards patient care and staff relationships seemed to be changing. In spite of the everyday pressures of general practice, there was a real willingness to rethink some of the traditional and stereotypical ways of relating to patients. The idea gaining ground was that teamwork could actually be a valuable adjunct to traditional ways of working with patients. Those with seemingly impossible problems would no longer need to be kept at arm's length. The GPs would be more aware of the true nature of their patients' anxieties and could provide emotional help at source. They need not feel trapped by the purely scientific limitations of their role. Instead it would be possible to extend the range of personal skills in the surgery by reassessing the nature of illness and understanding the hidden communications that pass between patients and their helpers. Where problems were potentially overwhelming, greater consideration would be given to the way in which responsibilities were shared among doctors and counsellors. The team, rather than the individual doctor, would temporarily share the responsibility, delegating one or two of its members to assess a family and report back to the group with their findings. Releasing the GP from the full weight of decision making and solution finding would have enormous benefits for patients and staff alike.

One result of this meeting was that the doctors and counsellors came to view each other with respect. This led to a reappraisal of the services offered by the surgery, without major resource implications. GP job satisfaction would be likely to improve under these conditions and cost savings would follow as an indirect result of patients feeling better understood. Unnecessary referrals to specialists, so common with multiproblem families, could be avoided.

Employment and accountability

The changing culture of primary care and increasing specialisation at local health centres has had an impact on patterns of employment. Three main methods of employment are as follows:

- Direct employment by fund-holding GPs.
- Secondment from the local NHS Trust, usually from departments of psychology or psychiatry, in which lines of accountability can run two ways:
  - to the GP for the standard of service they provide,
  - to their own managers back at the hospital, who aim to provide the highest standard of psychological services to the community.

- Semi-private practice, where counsellors are partly employed by the practice, but spend extra time in the surgery seeing surgery patients in a private capacity, usually for a reduced fee.

In all cases responsibility for patient care lies with the doctor, and therefore accountability should be to the doctor. Whatever the employment arrangements are, it is important to establish lines of accountability so that it is clear who is responsible for what if things go wrong. Professional accountability also lies with the counsellor's profession, which is responsible for ensuring the ongoing professional development of its members and has established procedures for handling ethical problems. The patient, the practitioner and the employer expect the counselling on offer to be based on the secure foundations of rigorous training and high standards. The counsellor in primary care may be part of an integrated mental health team, but in the primary care setting it is the GP who bears clinical and legal responsibility for every aspect of patient care taking place in health centre premises. It is the GP who is answerable to any charges of malpractice or other complaints, since the GP is the purchaser of the counsellor's services, not the patient. Assessing, selecting and referring, monitoring and, in particular, evaluating effectiveness all fall within the GP's orbit. Employment contracts have a direct influence on the professional relationship between doctor and counsellor and unless both sides are clear about the nature of their professional objectives, each will construe the other's tasks differently. To complicate matters further, as soon as a patient enters the picture a three-way relationship emerges, bringing with it all the inherent complications of triangular relationships. These need to be considered very carefully and require ongoing discussion and consultation in order that the professionals involved remain on-task in the care of their patients.

Group dynamics

Teamwork and the dynamics of teamwork constitute two overlapping key factors in primary care. Counsellors have a psychodynamic perspective of their patients, and in order to work effectively as team members they also need to bear in mind that groups and teams have dynamics operating within and between them.

Counsellors and GPs bring different characteristics to the workplace and these affect the dynamics that develop in the primary care team. Group dynamics invariably centre on issues of power and control, rivalry and competition, who has more and who has less. Possessiveness of the patient may play a part, no matter how committed teams may be in theory to joint working arrangements. These feelings can seriously undermine the efficiency of all groups, not least the primary care team. The corrosive influence of these dynamics can be averted through open and frank team discussions, and by the presence of strong leaders whose clear vision of the purpose of the team can inspire others. In reality this ideal is seldom met. GPs and counsellors like to get on with their work unimpeded by extraneous considerations. Everyone likes to operate within neat boundaries. Administration, management and leadership can be disliked because these activities take professionals away from direct patient care. Consequently one dynamic affecting the primary care team is avoidance of leadership and management by doctors and counsellors alike. These roles are given to others, for example practice managers, who may lack the authority to fulfil their roles adequately. In group practices doctors cannot avoid the issue of leadership. One of them will have to be appointed senior partner, even if on a rotating basis, to oversee the policies and practices of the surgery as a whole, including the integration of counselling into the general provision of services for patients.

Gender

It is more common for GPs to be male and for counsellors to be female. In the main this alliance can be described as a kind of 'marriage' that finds its reflection in the dominant-male/submissive-female stereotype. Primary care structures and the nature of the employment relationship lend themselves to this kind of male–female split, but may not always bring with it all the negative associations that this division implies. It may well be necessary for the GP to process the patient rather peremptorily, yet desirable that the counsellor be softer, slower and more nurturing. This division generally works successfully for all three parties involved. However, it is open to that traditional pitfall of marriage: the bullying, domineering male doctor and the compliant, passive, insecure female counsellor. Some responsibility for establishing and sustaining these polarities must lie with the socialisation inherent in their respective professional training programmes.

Training

Doctors are graduates with at least six years of undergraduate clinical, hospital-based training. Counsellors may emerge after far

shorter training programmes. They come from a variety of professional backgrounds, and for many counselling is their second or
third career. Their training is heavily theory-based, with the clinical
component rarely extending beyond six hours per week. Unlike
doctors, whose medical training emphasises diagnosis, rapid decision making, responsibility for decisions and active behaviour in the
treatment process, counsellors wait for their patients to reach
decisions at their own speed. They are more passive and less
concerned with diagnosis than they are with process and the
evolution of the patient and the patient–counsellor relationship.
Such vast differences in approach and attitude, learned during
training, have a significant influence on team dynamics.

Time

It is not uncommon to hear doctors and counsellors complaining
about each other's use of time. Doctors can become exasperated at
counsellors' extravagance with time. They fail to comprehend why
such long lead times for patient appointments are necessary, or to
see the point of repeated visits. All of these may be regarded as part
of a general tendency to lavish copious amounts of time as an
indulgence. They may not understand why counsellors insist on
their appointments lasting fifty minutes when theirs last ten on
average.

Split transference

Transference is rife in primary care settings and GPs and counsellors can be attributed the roles of 'good' and 'bad' parent. Patients
may play one off against the other to allay feelings of intolerable
ambivalence towards their doctor. Or they may lay all negative
feelings at the feet of their counsellors and discuss them critically
behind their backs. Counsellors would prefer their patients to talk to
them about any feelings they might have regarding the counselling
or the counsellor, and they do not understand why patients may
prefer to talk instead to their doctors. Counsellors need to understand the 'split transference' that goes on in general practice and the
primitive parental transferences that patients have with their doctors.

External referrals

Counsellors have different arrangements for referring patients to
outside sources of help. In some cases they make all the necessary
arrangements; in others GPs prefer to make the decisions. Where

this happens counsellors may feel marginalised, because the GPs do have the deciding role and their decision may be based on financial or other grounds. Counsellors' sense of identity and professional worth can be safeguarded and strengthened by having discussions and reaching an agreement on the parameters of authority for decision making.

Leadership and authority

The GP

GPs exercise leadership by drafting clear guidelines, job descriptions and personal specifications for the counsellors, and by becoming directly involved in the employment selection procedures. The fact that they have the right to hire and fire presupposes that GPs are moderately familiar with counselling and all that this entails: pre- and post-professional training; ongoing supervision of its practitioners; BAC qualification requirements; codes of practice, codes of ethics and the machinery to deal with any breach of ethics.

The counsellor

Counsellors also need to assume appropriate leadership responsibility. They are able to draw on the sense of professional identity acquired during training and on their status as members of a professional body, reinforced by their employment or secondment contracts. Counsellors usually exercise authority by attending to their patients' emotional and psychological needs, whatever obstacles there may be. In terms of practical hurdles, funding appropriate treatment for patients may require assertive advocacy by the counsellor. It is worth remembering that another facet of professional discipline may be the need to rein-in our own emotions.

CASE EXAMPLE: COPING WITH ANGER

A GP has taken much trouble to arrange an appointment for a patient at a specialist clinic. The GP is annoyed by the patient's failure to keep that appointment and she is reluctant to make another referral. The counsellor argues that because a child is involved, one more referral should be attempted. The GP is relieved that her irritation with the patient has abated and she makes a second referral.

Counsellors' authority as professionals means that they are answerable for their actions and omissions. Although overall legal responsibility for patient care rests with the employing GP, professional responsibility cannot be and should never be abdicated completely. Counsellors are expected to share fully in the deliberations and decisions of their teams, and to be responsible for the contributions they make to the team and for their work with patients. As responsible professionals, they monitor and evaluate their work with a view to improving standards and effectiveness. Authority and accountability are two key issues for counsellors. They are accountable to doctors in the same way that any service provider is to a purchaser. But they are also accountable to their own sense of professionalism, to their profession of counselling, and they must be dedicated to upholding standards and improving performance.

Summary
Several key professional issues have emerged out of the changing professional culture of primary care in the mid 1990s. Issues of confidentiality, communication and employment characterise the main aspects of the GP–counsellor relationship. Group dynamics or the dynamics of teamwork are an essential part of the practice's pool of skills. Supervision/consultation is vital in dealing with problems that can potentially impede effective work. In this litigious age, which has seen medicine redefined as business labouring under financial pressures, group dynamics have become more complicated than ever. These problems are often exacerbated when a GP does not work well with the newly affiliated disciplines in his or her practice, or when professional relationships between the practice, the health authority or other professional associations become fraught with tension.

9

DOES COUNSELLING WORK?

CASE EXAMPLE: RUTH

Ruth, an upset, tearful woman of 72, tells the practice counsellor about the death of her husband four weeks earlier. They were childless and had been married for 34 years. They were very happy together, she says. Her life now feels empty and futile. At home she cries without tears, but in the session she manages to shed tears. It is difficult to witness her loss. Ruth goes on to say that she wants to bring him back; at home she 'talks' to her deceased husband and thinks she is going mad. Everything they did, they did for each other; they had wonderful times together; they laughed together and they cared for each other. She starts talking about the night he died and she weeps even more. She was with him in the hospital and she describes his last moments in detail. At the end of the session Ruth says she is grateful for the opportunity to talk and readily accepts another appointment a fortnight later.

She returns for her second session, looking and feeling better. She still cries, but less so. She describes the alternative arrangements she is making in her life. They are happening slowly, but she is getting out more and meeting people, family and friends. She admits that her own mortality has been on her mind, but it has not dragged her down in despair. She realises that she still has a few years left and she wants to use them fruitfully. Ruth again expresses gratitude to her GP and to the counsellor for the opportunity to talk, which has helped her gain a different perspective on her loss and her future life. She says she does not feel the need to come again, but the counsellor reminds her that she may do so if she changes her mind.

How to evaluate counselling?

The above is an example of counselling in practice. Has it worked? Most would respond with an unqualified 'yes'. But how can success in counselling as a whole be evaluated? That is a far more complex matter. Whereas research findings of the early 1980s demonstrated a positive trend in favour of counselling in primary care (Ashurst and Ward, 1983; Martin and Mitchell, 1983; Balestieri *et al.* 1988), most of the recent research on effectiveness seems to reach depressingly negative and pessimistic conclusions. Repeated attempts to evaluate the positive effectiveness of counselling reveal little or no quantifiable benefit to patients. Clearly these findings do not reflect Ruth's experience. How should the effectiveness of her two interviews be evaluated? Should Ruth be asked to complete a questionnaire, and would that be sufficient? Must we ask one hundred Ruths to comment on their satisfaction levels and their symptom reduction? There is ample evidence that counselling services are widely held in high regard and that patients such as Ruth find them helpful and effective.

It has been suggested that this gap between experience and evaluation is the result of methodological problems in the research (Pringle, 1993). It is obvious that qualitative studies should replace quantitative research in a counselling context. Outmoded quantitative research paradigms are bound to produce results that demonstrate little or no benefit. Among the many criticisms levelled at poorly evaluated counselling is Hughes' (1993) contention that counselling services neither provide GPs with specific, tangible benefits nor help to reduce their workload. Savings on the prescribing budget are unimpressive. Foulger (1993) counters this argument: 'should the suffering addressed by counselling be considered insufficiently tangible and therefore undeserving of more than a modicum of NHS resources?' House argues that were it possible to identify and quantify all the relevant variables, then:

> counselling would unambiguously be shown to be a highly cost-effective form of health-care intervention. There are intrinsic reasons why it is impossible to make the kind of objective evaluation of counselling that is demanded by the modern scientific paradigm and the logic of market forces (House, 1993, unpublished paper)

We believe that there is little purpose in seeking to define the effectiveness of counselling in primary care by using traditional research methods. We argue that research paradigms appropriate to psychodynamic models should be developed in order to appreciate the contribution of counselling to primary care. These paradigms, as Ruth's case demonstrates so effectively, must have their roots in qualitative research. Ruth's experience would be lost in a medical quantitative paradigm, which establishes objective knowledge of cause and effect through the testing of specific hypotheses against phenomena in the empirical world. Quantification is seen as a *sine qua non* of the medical sciences' paradigm because it renders theoretical concepts observable, manipulable and testable.

Using qualitative methodology, an evaluation of Ruth's encounter can be reached through an appreciation of the patient's experience of the counselling process and the mental and emotional changes occasioned by it. This interpretative task cannot be accomplished by observing the patient as a mechanism geared to respond to certain conditions in regular ways; rather the researcher has to 'get inside' the patient *and* the social context surrounding the patient's crisis. This requires a kind of understanding called, in the qualitative research literature, *Verstehen,* in which, through an empathic and imaginative identification with the patient, the researcher makes sense of what the patient is doing or experiencing. Counsellors' understanding of their patients' minds, history and social milieu, involves concepts expressed by and located in language. Through language, counsellors can demonstrate that patients are not isolated interpreters of their worlds.

The patient can only be understood in terms of what is happening in *her or his* life, not by grouping her or him into a large random sample. To be sure, Ruth's experience of counselling can be classified as the experience of an elderly, recently bereaved widow, and Ruth as a statistic will form the basis of cost projections for the NHS purse and the planning of services for an aging population in which many become single again. However we are arguing for a totally new research paradigm; a method of evaluation that is in sympathy with and appropriate to a holistic healing approach where the less tangible qualities of human experience are paramount (House, 1993). In an encounter where the counsellor enters into discourse with the patient and attempts to reveal the shape of the patient's cognitive world, interpretation and empathy are key qualities, not predictional control. Hence counsellors insist there is an urgent need for heuristic techniques and participant observation. Few doctors currently share this view. Since career advancement opportunities for doctors are based on their publishing statistical research, there is bound to be resistance to qualitative evaluation from all but a few

(Brook, 1967; Graham and Sher, 1976; Balint, 1986; Elder, 1987; Balint, 1993). Counsellors proclaim with pride that their models of understanding their patients' minds, life experiences, health and the meaning of symptoms differ radically from that of doctors, but often complement them. They should protest with equal vigour that their research methods and models must, by their very nature, differ radically from those applied by the medical profession. Counsellors need to be more proactive in promoting and conducting research using paradigms that are suited to the ethics and practice of counselling, and disseminate their findings widely.

Current definitions of the term 'research' (Bateman and Holmes, 1995) emphasise measurement, the rigorous use of controls, statistical manipulation of data and replicability. It seems to us that too much counselling research is based on outcome studies looking at the results of counselling treatment, and that there is not enough process research that monitors what happens in the counselling process itself. Fonagy (1993, p. 577) criticises process research methods because of their emphasis on anecdotal clinical data, which is dependent on an 'outmoded epistemological paradigm of enumerative inductionism', in other words, generalising from a number of examples. Many attempts to research psychodynamic processes fall short of the standards usually required by orthodox methods. Conversely many counsellors disregard contemporary research as largely irrelevant to their day-to-day work. Some argue that the world of feelings and fantasies can only be reached by introspection and is therefore inherently unresearchable.

We would reject these arguments on the grounds that research into counselling is necessary to reassure counsellors that their work is an effective and useful treatment for psychological distress. Research also helps sift fact from myth and so enables counselling to scrutinise and refine itself in order to discard what is unworkable. Since counselling in primary care is a publicly funded form of treatment, it will be required to prove itself.

Qualitative research in other disciplines is now well-established with trained practitioners, high standards of work and codes of ethics. In market research, for example, there is an Association of Qualitative Research Practitioners with a membership approaching 1000. Methods usually involve semistructured or unstructured individual in-depth interviews and, most commonly, what are now called focus groups, where seven or eight people are interviewed as a group, led by a skilled moderator. Sometimes, interviews are carried out with families or friendship pairs. Morgan

(1988, p. 12) sees the focus group as a unique tool: 'providing data and insights that only this forum can provide'. In our view, these are the techniques we must employ if we are to move forward and begin to evaluate counselling in primary care more adequately.

Redefining the problem

The Counselling in Primary Care Trust has made funds available for university-validated primary care programmes at MSc level (see Appendix A). Topics covered in the training include core areas of interprofessional collaboration, medical models of health and illness, personal and professional development and brief models of therapy. Other elements such as loss and bereavement, psychosexual problems, post-traumatic stress disorders and destructive family systems are also offered. These courses also focus on research. Curtis-Jenkins (1996) highlights the difficulties of conducting research in the UK compared with the USA, where information technology (IT) allows researchers to track patients accurately through a managed health care system subject to continuous audit and evaluation routines. He lays the blame with those civil servants who are responsible for commissioning the IT and those NHS managers who tailored it, neither of whom have more than scant understanding of the counselling process.

However there are flaws in Curtis-Jenkins' arguments. He suggests that changes in counselling practice and values must keep step with medicine; that counselling practice will increasingly resemble medical practice, with its 'good-quality research', a code for the number-based, quantitative research much-loved by doctors. There is little acknowledgment that counselling has been welcomed into primary care *because* it is fundamentally different from medicine in approach, philosophy, values and behaviour. Counselling has been deliberately invited into primary care as a diversified resource, seeking not 'cures', but understanding. To merge the evaluation of counselling's effectiveness with medical models is to deny its *raison d'être*.

CASE EXAMPLE: AISHA

Aisha, an Asian woman of 38, is referred by her GP to explore the possibility of psychological causes for a pain in her left arm. This pain first appeared when she was 16. It persisted and grew steadily worse and is now impairing her ability to write her answers in the civil service examinations, which are her prime reason for being in this country. Over the last two years the pain has become a tremor. Aisha has been sent for numerous tests, the outcome of which were all negative, and she is becoming upset at the specialists' implication that her pain is imaginary.

Aisha has lived in this country with her three children for ten years. Her husband lives in their home country, visiting her and the children in the UK once a year. She says she has passed most of her examinations, but has failed one paper every year, necessitating an extension of her stay each time. She is one of eight children from a lower-middle-class family. Her father is a strict disciplinarian and her mother is 'hypercritical'. They are in perpetual conflict. She believes her mother does not like her and she has no one in the family to talk to about her feelings.

The counsellor tells Aisha that serious personal conflicts can, in certain situations, become 'internalised' and lead to physical symptoms. Aisha looks surprised and she asks whether the pain in her arm could be related to earlier family tensions. She says that she was surprised when the counsellor asked about her husband and her family. Throughout all her medical tests no inquiries have been made about her personal history. The patient wants a further appointment.

At the next visit Aisha continues to express her bewilderment at the counsellor's emphasis on her personal and social life. She prefers to concentrate specifically on the pain in her arm. After the first interview she thought about the possible 'emotional' aspects of her pain, but remains sceptical. She then goes on to say that her marriage is 'dead', and that since they live in different countries and barely communicate, she is happy for the separation to continue while she studies, and wants a divorce as soon as her studies are over.

Aisha's behaviour and attitude would be unacceptable in her home country, where women are repressed socially and cultu-rally. Realising this, Aisha had become frightened and bewildered but coped by suppressing her feelings and wishes. The counsellor senses a connection between Aisha's wish to keep her husband at bay and failing her exams; the pain and the tremor are responses to these emotional states, to the point where they have become a form of hysterical conversion syndrome.

At the end of the session Aisha says there is something further she would like to discuss and asks for another appointment. At the next session she is agitated and suspicious about notes being kept. She bursts into uncontrollable tears, asks for water, apologises for her distress and then speaks in detail of the sexual abuse that she and her sisters suffered at the hands of her stepbrother over a number of years. She goes on to say that her mother colluded with the abuse, until eventually the whole family fell apart when the patient's older sister revealed the truth.

Aisha feels intense relief at revealing this part of her history. She has never spoken about it before and she says she can see how psychological pain could become transformed into physical pain. In the next two sessions she eagerly shows how she is regaining the use of her arm. She had been disturbed as well as relieved by disclosing her past history, and in the next session she speaks of her guilty feelings at not having done more to protect her sisters from her predatory stepbrother. She also expresses angry feelings towards her mother, whose negligence she feels was responsible for the family's traumatic disintegration.

The patient is seen four more times prior to her final exams so that she has an opportunity to discuss her feelings again and move on to focus fully on her exams without relying on those unconscious defences that might lead her to fail again. Her arm does not let her down and she passes her exams. Afterwards she files for divorce, gets a good job in the civil service and continues to live in the UK with her children.

How can one evaluate a case like Aisha's? Were her symptoms removed? How do we rate the outcome? Poor? Moderate? Good? The fact is that her symptoms eased sufficiently to enable her to pass her exams and face life constructively. Should clearly calculable savings to the NHS also be costed in, since there was no longer any need for expensive investigations with specialists? If patients truly regard their health centres as places to go to receive help with life's problems (these patients have an illness, but no organic disease), where clarification of feelings in relation to self and life events can take place, how are we to cost these? So many sessions at £x per session equals what?

While we are not shy of Curtis-Jenkins' 'good-quality research' in evaluating the contribution of counselling to primary care, we believe that research in counselling should be based on sound, rigorous, qualitative research principles to reflect cases such as Aisha's. Counselling research activity must apply unstructured, non-numerical material such as protocol studies, discourse work, interviewing and participant observation, where we talk to patients about their experiences of counselling. Research methods should be tailored to the assessment of particular problems, not the other way around.

Like Curtis-Jenkins, we agree that endless 'does counselling work?' studies must become creatures of the past, and in their place counsellors need to set up research projects consistent with the counselling enterprise itself: 'knowing about the person who has a disease, rather than knowing about the disease that the person has' (House, 1993). The gathering and analysis of non-numerical, experiential data is appropriate for the counselling discipline because it is a sensitive tool that frees researchers to explore the multiple interpretations and meanings that may be placed upon the patient's thoughts and behaviour by the patient and by the GP (Lincoln and Guba, 1985).

The cost-effectiveness of counselling

Evaluation of counselling usually focuses on questions of cost efficiency. Does it work? If so, can it be shown to do so in accordance with the government's commitment to cost analysis and value for money? In the light of this rationale, counselling is usually evaluated in terms of (1) whether or not it works, and with which patients; and (2) whether, when measured against other forms of treatment, counselling costs less and is the most effective option. Decisions about counselling are not easy to take and economic analysis is a blunt instrument when it comes to providing information about the differing costs and effects. Selection criteria may rest on the greatest number of outcomes for a certain fixed cost (or budget), or on the attainment of a particular target outcome at the lowest possible price.

In *Promoting Better Health* (DHSS, 1987) the government placed primary care services at the front line of the National Health Service (Rowland and Tolley, 1995), so general practice was meant to accept a wide range of professions operating within it and funds were made available to remunerate them. These plans provided the required impetus for the expansion of counselling services in primary care. However the expansion was ill-timed, coinciding with an era of budgetary constraints and competitive choices between different health care professionals. Economic analysis helps clarify aims and objectives. A system of health care that keeps budgetary control at the local level, requires detailed financial information on how well a particular service is faring: is it doing what it purports to do more cheaply and as effectively as a similar service? Put another way, counsellors and counselling are subject to the same financial constraints as all other disciplines in primary care.

Many of the researchers mentioned above do acknowledge that counselling is difficult to assess (Waydenfeld and Waydenfeld, 1980; Martin and Mitchell, 1983; Balestieri et al., 1988). As medical time and medication are the most costly units in primary care, researchers are inclined to investigate whether counselling input leads to a significant reduction in attendance and prescription rates. Waydenfeld and Waydenfeld (1980) and Koch (1979) showed that attendance at the surgery and the number of prescriptions issued fell by 31 per cent in the six-month period following the conclusion of a counselling intervention. Patients, doctors and counsellors registered high levels of satisfaction with the provision of on-site counselling, although few doctors thought that their workloads had decreased (Ives, 1979; Anderson and Hasler, 1979; Ashurst and Ward, 1983). The workload of some doctors actually increased, although this was largely because of the extra time devoted to discussions with counsellors. This alone reinforces our belief that cost reduction in itself is incomplete in determining the usefulness of counselling.

In our view budgetary considerations should never be the only yardstick for measuring value; counselling in primary care must also *promote good practice*. There are cases – such as multiproblem families, mental illness, alcoholism, or where children are involved – where it is unrealistic to expect one person or one agency working alone to manage the multifaceted problems affecting these patients (Calnan, 1991; Hornby, 1993). Here a multidisciplinary input is called for, and it is a *sine qua non* that doctor and counsellor will need to talk to each other to devise treatment plans and iron out conflicts between them. All this takes time and involves extra cost, but this cost must be seen as an investment in building an efficient infrastructure capable of functioning as a unit. Such costs are not easily measured against the benefits of working together to contain some of the more distressed patients.

Freeman and Button (1984) found a marked reduction in the rates of attendance and psychotrophic drug prescription in the six months after counselling treatment, compared with the six months leading up to it. However they also noticed that attendance and prescription rates for the whole practice fell overall during the period of the study. The data was patchy and they discovered that presentation of one type of psycho-social problem tended to be concentrated in a relatively short period, 'a worst year', rather than being evenly distributed over the whole six years. They conclude that it may be difficult to interpret reductions in consulting and prescribing rates unless contemporary trends for the whole practice are taken into account.

Freeman and Button's findings make a case for any cost-effective analysis to take a system-based approach, namely an analysis of the relationship between doctor and patient, counsellor and patient and the practice as a whole, and the lines of enquiry must be consistent with that approach. For instance what, if any, were the systemic reasons for patient attendance and prescription rates? Was the practice in trouble? Was there conflict between the practice partners? To what extent did the counsellor's presence in the practice ease the anxiety of its GPs? Was the 'worst year' phenomenon a reflection of the practice's worst year or the patients'? Should we measure cost-effectiveness in terms of improved GP confidence in dealing with psycho-social problems as a result of the presence of a counsellor in the practice?

It is commonly accepted that professions and organisations whose role is to deal with stress and breakdown are likely to be subject to stress and breakdown themselves, a kind of psychological cross-infection. Protection from the effects of these stresses and trauma can lead to dysfunctional defences in organisations and in the individual, and ultimately cause the level of professional performance to deteriorate. The system becomes inefficient. Costs, as measured by dissatisfied patients, staff illness rates, absenteeism, general unhappiness and low staff morale at work, all escalate. Attempts to help the situation without taking account of the existence of stress swirling around the organisation are merely tinkering with the problem.

Stress and cost-effectiveness

Uncontained stress carries costs and its implications are felt in ripples throughout the practice. Witnessing and experiencing intense emotions, negative dependency and infinite need on a daily basis will, according to Obholzer (1988, p. 119), 'result in disproportionately heavy wear and tear in both human and physical resources'. One response to this spiralling stress is to draft in ever more help, which is stress-generating in itself. Another response is for GP and counsellor to 'split' and work separately, but this only serves to exacerbate the stress level. A third defence is to retreat behind a smokescreen of statistics and figures:

> financial [goals] take no account of the quality of the service to the patient. It is more comfortable for researchers and managers to make decisions without consulting clinicians and patients, because that way, they are effectively cut-off from the human consequences of their actions. In the short-term, there may be effective change, but the long-term prognosis of a system that operates in this split-off manner will be a costly one. It is psychologically easier to avoid patient pain and instead focus on budgets (ibid., p. 121).

We believe a psychodynamic approach to counselling in primary care should go hand in hand with a psychodynamic understanding of health care systems, the stresses they generate and the way they are costed. It is not possible to understand and address the issue of cost in any system that operates in ignorance of unconscious processes at work.

CASE EXAMPLE: PROBLEM FAMILIES

A GP approaches the practice counsellor to discuss a general problem in the practice: six families who are heavy users of the surgery's services. The GP is particularly concerned because the children of all six families are sometimes presented at the practice on a weekly basis. The GP is feeling desperate and helpless because he finds it difficult to confront the parents, usually the mothers, with the view that presenting their children is pointless as the children have nothing wrong with them. Worse still, he can seldom resist the parents' pressure to refer their children to specialists. The mothers offer the GP apparently knowledgeable diagnostic assessments of their children's conditions and are clear about the specialist to whom they wish to be referred. The GP says guiltily that more often than not, he simply acquiesces to the parents' wishes and refers their children to a specialist, knowing that he is making a fool of himself and that he will eventually hear from the specialist that there is nothing wrong with the child. The GP wishes that he had more skill in understanding and dealing with these families. The counsellor offers to see two of the families as a way of helping the GP to manage them.

This is arranged and the counsellor sees the families. He finds that both have repeatedly presented their prepubescent sons to the GP, requesting various intelligence and psychiatric assessments because they claim that the boys are negative, argumentative, lack concentration and drive, neglect their homework, are socially isolated and never wash or tidy their rooms. The counsellor sees these families several times each over some months. Like the GP, the counsellor feels intense pressure to agree with the parents that their sons are psychiatrically ill. They want him to convey this to the GP, so that referral to a child psychiatrist can be arranged. The counsellor refuses to comply with their wishes but draws attention to the families' need to find someone who will 'carry the sick parts' of the family system. In both cases this is the presence of a severe, life-threatening illness in one the parents.

The counsellor's approach in both cases is to see the families in a variety of configurations: parents with all their children; parents with one child who is the 'designated' patient; parents together and individually. He resists their attempts to force their sons into psychiatric categories and instead focuses on their denial of the effect the parental illness is having on their marriages and their relationships with their children. He says that they are 'putting' their own feelings of helpless rage onto their sons, and the passive partners are colluding with their dominant partners because psychiatric treatment of their sons seems to offer more hope of success than they can expect with their partners' long and debilitating illness.

These discussions, painful and enraging as they are, help the parents in both families to look for the first time at the roles they have taken up in their marriages and at what they are really doing to each other and to themselves. They are puzzled, angry and sad. They rage at the counsellor for daring to redefine their problems and they rage at their GP for daring to refer them to the counsellor, thereby removing what has become a comfortable denial of their real problems.

In the event the rate of both families' attendance at the surgery falls to normal levels. They stop requesting psychiatric assessment for their sons and the submissive spouses adopt more responsible attitudes and roles in relation to their sick partners.

In addition to the constructive rearrangement of relationships in these families, the effect of these changes on the GP and the practice is worth noting. Firstly, the GP feels strengthened in his capacity to work with these 'difficult' patients, rather than to submit to all their demands or to remove them from his list. Secondly, the GP learns new approaches and skills that are translated into his work with other multiproblem families. Thirdly, the financial cost in terms of visits to the practice and referrals to specialists is contained within normal limits.

This example illustrates the variety of benefits that can accrue to all those involved. For the patients and their families there were obvious clinical benefits, for the professionals a reduction in stress and an increase in morale, and for the health centre's budget, significant financial savings. These parents achieved greater aware-ness and insight into the hidden meanings behind the physical expression of their mental states and were shown how to contain their unreasonable demands and behaviour.

Summary

Members of the primary care team are often 'container's, metabolising the anxieties projected onto them, and to have the best chance of operating at an optimum level there has to be an ongoing dialogue between the team members. All concerned need to be in touch with the difficulties of the task and their relative powerlessness radically to alter the pattern of life, something patients desperately want them to do.

Research into counselling should take account of this 'containing' function of professionals and organisations. Limiting research aims to specific behavioural and symptomatic improvements in individual patients, important though this is, is insufficient. Main (1989b p. 206) said that patients only stand a chance 'when their doctors are in good shape'. 'Good shape' includes being aware of the traps that some patients set to force their helpers to be what they simply cannot be and to deliver to them what they cannot provide for themselves.

This chapter has emphasised the need for an epistemologically improved paradigm for evaluating counselling in primary care. We are aware, however, that in making recommendations for change we have not set out specific guidelines on how these changes should be implemented. At the most basic level, we support East's position that counsellors must join the front benches of the political arena and fight their corner:

If counselling in medical settings has a future as a healing process in its own right, its leaders will need to be able to take part in the political arenas where (political) will is determined. In these circumstances, being well-meaning is insufficient. Sophisticated political skills and strategies are needed in order to be heard and taken seriously (East, 1995, p. 137).

In more practical terms, counsellors and GPs should add a *research orientation* to the other elements of their job, described throughout this book. This means the establishment of a database of patients referred to and seen by the counsellor: demographic details, types of problem and forms of intervention used. This information will represent the fulcrum of future research and evaluation developments, particularly if local practices pool their information and research resources.

Research should therefore consider the contributions to patient health as a whole that come from having counselling located in the surgery. Anything that increases the psychological resources and improves the morale and efficiency of its staff must surely be welcomed. A different way of thinking is required. Its benefits may have implications for everyone. To demonstrate these benefits, new research methods will have to be used that allow patients to register their reactions while engaged in, or immediately following, the counselling experience. Such is the nature of the counselling encounter that personal responses are crucial if widely felt benefits are to shine through. How else are we to assess the value of a treatment that is so intimate, human and personal?

APPENDIX A:
KEY TERMS AND CONCEPTS

Introduction

Psychodynamic, as the word indicates, refers to the psyche and implies a propensity for movement and change. It has its origins in the psychoanalytic movement, begun and shaped by Freud over one hundred years ago. Although what might be called the 'apostolic era' of psychoanalysis is now over (Bateman and Holmes, 1995), its theory and practice continue to influence culture all over the world. Whilst it is beyond the scope of this book to provide the reader with a comprehensive overview of the many different models of the mind that can be included under the heading of psychoanalytic theory, it may be helpful to summarise briefly some of the main principles that influence our own work and are relevant in primary care. The reader will find an excellent account of the development of psychoanalytic models of the mind in Chapter 2 of *Introduction to Psychoanalysis* by Bateman and Holmes (1995).

As an institution in which to work, a GP practice has particular characteristics that permit the evolution of different sets of relationships: between health professionals and patients; between the different health professionals who work in the practice; and between the health professionals and their managers. A model of the mind that places its central emphasis on *relationships* is therefore likely to be of most relevance (although not the only model to be relevant) to a GP or counsellor interested in the application of psychodynamic principles to the understanding of both the nature of the practice as an institution and the relationships that develop within it.

Psychoanalytic models today have come a long way from Freud's original *drive theory,* and because of the overlap and interaction between the many different contemporary models, some confusion is inevitable. For us it is *object relations* theory as developed in much of the published work of Balint, Bion, Fairbairn, Guntrip, Klein and Winnicott that provides the most relevant conceptual framework for thinking about work in primary care. Central to this theory is the belief that human beings' prime motivation is to form relationships with other people rather than, as Freud originally thought, the instinctual search for pleasure and avoidance of pain. In object relations theory, each person is seen to have an internal world containing a core self, versions of other people perceived by this core self (internal objects) and a network of relationships between these internal objects. The essential character of this matrix is determined by the quality of the infant's earliest experiences of communication and empathy with its mother and other family members, including such experiences as feeding, holding, looking/being looked at and so on. The matrix is likely to be played out in subsequent intimate relationships at different stages of life and will affect the nature of the anxieties, vulnerabilities and defences in people's relationships.

Unconscious processes

The concept of the *unconscious* is central to psychoanalytic theory and it was Freud who first wrote about the unconscious in mental life. The term may be used to describe mental contents that are inaccessible to the ego and also to denote a psychic place, a part of the mental apparatus that has its own character, laws and functions. With the development in psychoanalysis away from structures of the mind towards relationships and the value of understanding the meaning of communications between people, it is now more common to talk about *unconscious processes* rather than the unconscious.

Freud tended to see people as beset with constant struggles and conflicts that they defend against by repressing incompatible or unacceptable feelings and thoughts. He believed that psychological maturity involves the strengthening of the ego, so that an individual's perception of external reality (the reality principle) can be freed from distortion by pressures from internal conflicts. Thus the growth of the ego gives better expression to instincts in a way that modifies stress in the personality as a whole.

Jung regarded the unconscious as a repository of repressed, infantile personal experiences but also as a locus of psychological activity which differed from and was more objective than personal experience since it related directly to the phylogenetic, instinctual bases of the human race (Samuels *et al.*, 1986, p. 155). He called the former (repressed, infantile experience) the *personal unconscious* and the latter the *collective unconscious*. Jung believed that the contents of the collective unconscious operate independently of the ego at a deeper layer of the mind than the personal unconscious; that they have never been in consciousness and that they reflect archetypal processes, that is, they are innate and common to all mankind and appear in culture as universal motifs. Contemporary analytical psychologists view the contents of the collective unconscious and the personal unconscious as connected at all levels (Williams, 1963). Whilst Jung, like Freud, placed value on the development of ego-consciousness, he was particularly interested in the unconscious aim of the psyche as individuation and realisation of the full potential of the self.

Mechanisms of defence

Frustration, pain, rage, hate and fears about survival, especially in objectively unfavourable circumstances, are emotions that enter all our lives and must be tolerated alongside more pleasurable emotions such as hope, love and excitement. If the former significantly outbalance the latter at any time, then it is likely that individuals will erect defences to protect themselves against these unpleasant affects. One of the main tasks for the counsellor when seeing a new patient is to assess the nature and rigidity of the patient's defences, and to be able to distinguish between those defences that are necessary for the patient's survival and those that may interfere with healthy development and lead to the appearance of symptoms.

Classical psychoanalysis, with its emphasis on intrapsychic phenomena, postulates that *conflict is* the central psychic struggle and views *repression as* the main defence mechanism. Unacceptable wishes or emotions remain unconscious or disguised by the unconscious mechanism of repression. Object relations theory and analytical psychology have a broader conception of defence mechanisms as an attempt on the part of the individual to *protect core aspects of the self,* particularly those aspects that are vulnerable to damage (Winnicott, 1965; Lambert, 1981; Kohut, 1984; Fordham, 1985). Other authors, including Klein (1946), Rosenfeld (1964), Meltzer (1968) and Steiner (1982), put forward another view of defences, highlighting how in some personalities, such as those where borderline and narcissistic structures are evident, defence mechanisms can become a *fixed part of the personality structure.*

In the following table, Bateman and Holmes (1995) helpfully divide defence mechanisms into three main types: primitive/immature, neurotic and mature. It is important to stress that all the defences they mention are likely to emerge at different times in any one individual, but they will only become pathological, or part of a more total pattern, if used persistently.

Primitive/immature	Neurotic	Mature
Autistic fantasy	Condensation	Humour
Devaluation	Denial	Sublimation
Idealisation	Displacement	
Passive-aggression	Dissociation	
Projection	Externalisation	
Projective identification	Identification with aggressor	
Splitting	Intellectualisation	
	Isolation	
	Rationalisation	
	Reaction Formation	
	Regression	
	Repression	
	Reversal	
	Somatisation	
	Undoing	

Source: Bateman and Holmes (1995). Reproduced with permission.

This list is based on psychoanalytic principles that place great emphasis on the ego, but it omits work from the field of analytical psychology based on the writings of C. G. Jung. A contemporary analytical psychologist, Michael Fordham (1974), describes a set of defences to be added to Holmes and Bateman's list, which he calls *defences of the self*. The self is of central importance to analytical psychology, larger altogether than the ego, and Fordham illustrates how the self, just as much as the ego, has mechanisms of defence. Usually, if defences of the self are evident the patient has been the victim of extreme early environmental failure, and these defences are the patient's attempt to protect him- or herself against excessive fears of disintegration, abandonment or annihilation, connected with huge disappointments and unmet expectations. Such patients will be seen regularly by counsellors working in the surgery and a knowledge of these mechanisms is vital.

Projective identification

Projective identification is an important mechanism of defence; it is the core stuff of psychoanalysis and counselling as it operates at the heart of the relationship between the two people (or more) involved in the counselling relationship. The reader will have noticed that it is listed above as a primitive or immature defence mechanism, but its usefulness as a means by which some of the processes in primary care may be observed suggests it deserves a section to itself.

Projection involves attributing to others feelings that are actually our own, for example when patients are ill it is common to attribute excessive hopes for recovery to the doctor. *Identification* refers to a process where self-representations formed during the early stages of life can develop with time and maturity, for example a patient who arrives at the practice with chest pains on or near the anniversary of the death of his father from a heart attack.

Klein (1946) described *projective identification* as a fantasy in which bad parts of the infantile self are split off from the rest of the self and projected into the mother. As a result infants feel that their mother has 'become' the bad parts of themselves. Klein conceived of this as a defence. Today the mechanism is not necessarily seen to be defensive but will often function as a communication. It refers to an unconscious interpersonal interaction in which the recipients of a projection react to it in such a way that their own feelings are affected: they unconsciously identify with the projected feelings. For example patients who complain to the GP about poor service may be projecting feelings about their neglectful parents. These projections may be (unconsciously) intended to make the doctor feel guilty as a way of compensating for unexpressed or unexpressable anger towards their parents.

Bateman and Holmes (1995) outline three distinct processes involved in the communicative aspects of projective identification: first, as already stated, it is an *interactive phenomenon,* the recipient of the projection may be induced to feel or act in ways that originate with the projection. Second, by extension, projective identification becomes a *mutual process* where projector and recipient interact with each other unconsciously and the recipient is in danger of enacting the feelings of the projector. Third, following the ideas of Bion (1961), there is a 'positive' form of projective identification underlying *empathy*, which may help the recipient to 'detoxify' feelings from the projector and return them in a more benign form.

CASE EXAMPLE: PASSING ON THE PROBLEM

When members of the primary care team project their sadness and depression about the death of a female patient, with whom they have been closely involved, onto the senior partner at a practice meeting, the senior partner feels the sadness and depression as if they are his own. This state of mind, in which other people's feelings are experienced as one's own, is called the *countertransference* (see below). The practice nurse, who was involved with this patient during her illness, acts out the countertransference, deriving from projected feelings, when she begins to experience similar physical symptoms. The true source of the symptoms is likely to remain obscure unless she can find some way of realising that she has become caught up in a countertransference to a projective process. The mechanism of projective identification can operate powerfully in a group setting when, for example, a staff member is 'forced' to leave as the recipient of unwanted feelings that the rest of the staff would prefer not to own.

Institutional defences

It is possible to divide defence mechanisms into two types, the personal, as discussed above, and the institutional. Obholzer (1994, p. 87) believes they are usually related as 'staff members with individual defences "fitting" those of the institution are more likely to remain, while those whose individual defences are out of tune with the institution leave'.

Anxieties at work are likely to lead to institutional defences in the form of structures and practices that help defend the staff from anxiety. Some threats come from outside, for example when an organisation is at risk of closure or, in the case of primary care, experiencing a process of change resulting from external pressure. Others come from within, in the form of threats to self-esteem, capacity to do the job or group cohesiveness. Sometimes the different types of threat are involved in a subtle interplay.

Menzies Lyth (1988), writing about her famous study of the nursing profession in 1959, realised that many organisations in the helping professions tend to build up ways of protecting themselves against the anxiety of the life and death nature of the work they do. She believes that primitive anxieties are always present in any organisation or social structure. Influenced by the writings of Klein and Bion, she explored how the very structure of an institution can be seen as a form of defence, designed to avoid or minimise personal experiences of doubt, guilt, anxiety and uncertainty. However at times the structure is actually antisupportive to staff, and may negatively affect the work:

the need of the members of the organisation to use it in the struggle against anxiety leads to the development of socially structured defence mechanisms, which appear as elements in the organisation's structure, culture and mode of functioning (Menzies Lyth, 1988, p. 50).

It is possible to point to several different defences that protect staff against anxiety and uncertainty in primary care:

- The short, ten-minute consultation, for all its practical advantages, could be seen as a means by which GPs protect themselves from the emotional impact of involvement with their patients' psychological problems.
- 'Busyness' is surely a good example of a defence against anxiety and uncertainty.
- The requirement for good medical diagnoses and quick decisions can reinforce a more generally defensive atmosphere of 'action' rather than 'reflection' and avoidance of any space for thinking about the meaning of things.
- The new, bottom-up model in the NHS has led to an increasing need for GPs to spend a considerable amount of time in negotiating with outside managers and politicians and some denial of the decrease in emotional resources now available for patients.
- Counsellors trained to do individual counselling in a private setting may protect themselves from facing the complexities of work in a primary care setting by adhering to over-rigid methods of work.
- There is neglect of the huge, often unconscious, psychological impact that death or near-death experiences have on patients, their relatives and the staff (Obholzer, 1994).

There is a universal pull towards the use of groups to meet personal needs, rather than to further the task for which the group exists, and we will inevitably become caught up in unconscious group and institutional processes. An awareness of our personal failures and a reflective attitude towards our own feelings, as well as those of other members of our work teams, is likely to help the organisation to remain aware of its defensive structures and to maintain a thoughtful, non-judgmental stance.

Gordon Lawrence (1994) has talked about the paradigm shift in management consultancy from the *politics of salvation* to the *politics of revelation* (see Chapter 2 on the doctor–counsellor relationship). His ideas are also relevant to the primary care environment. By the 'politics of salvation', he means a culture where we work in a way that is dissociated from our environment, where change is imposed from the outside on individuals or systems holding power – through a missionary zeal aimed at conversion, rescue or cure – and creates a culture of dependency. He believes we are moving slowly towards the 'politics of revelation' where, with the arrival of information technology, there is now a greater emphasis on mutuality and support between role-holders, rather than competition, conflict and aggression. Access to more information means that transformation may now come from inside the person or system, and comes about when there is a revelation among people about the truth of their situation. In a Winnicottian sense, there is, he thinks, now more space between organisations, where generativity and innovation are possible and meaning can be found.

Transference and countertransference

Patients are bound to have an effect on both doctors and counsellors, and it is essential that both learn how to distinguish between what belongs to the patient and what to themselves. Hopefully, with experience it becomes possible to take on board the painful, inner problem of a patient in a repaired form whereby the patient can then understand and integrate it in a creative way. At times, however, the power of the patient impairs our capacity to reflect on what is happening and this can lead to *action* as a substitute for *thought*. Here we are in the area of transference and counter-transference phenomena.

Transference

The classical view of transference was that it was a resistance to treatment and a contaminating or distorting factor that analysis should iron out (Freud, 1895). It was seen as a process that occurred during treatment, where patients unconsciously transferred onto the analyst strong feelings previously experienced in relation to significant others. Understanding these connections was thought to uncover and make possible the working through of early childhood trauma.

There is now general agreement that transference is found within all relationships and also within our attitudes to institutions. Transference is now seen more widely and positively as a process evoked in present-day relationships, which allows the emergence of new, latent meanings to be played out within those relationships. The idea that infantile neurosis is the only explanation for adult pathology no longer holds much water (Bateman and Holmes, 1995). Bollas (1987) also sees transference as a fundamentally new experience in which aspects of psychic life that have not been previously 'thought' can be given time and space. He coined the term *the unthought known* to describe this potential.

Bateman and Holmes (1995) refer to a number of 'special forms' of transference that have emerged through work with more disturbed patients, such as those with borderline or narcissistic problems as well as those with severe psychiatric disorders. They talk firstly of *self-object transference*, where patients who have experienced failure in mirroring in childhood and are lacking in self-esteem hope the helper will see them as special, and may require a mirroring or supportive response from the helper, rather than premature interpretations, in order to nurture some growth in self-esteem. They refer to a *psychotic transference* as potentially occurring when patients are unable to imagine that the helper might be available to care for them, as by implication they have obliterated from their minds the helper as a thinking being. In other situations it can refer to actual transient psychotic symptoms, which may appear during treatment when patients are faced with an intolerable amount of pain.

Finally, there is reference to the *erotic transference*, where the patient develops an erotic attachment to the helper. Bateman and Holmes believe that if treated sensitively, erotic and loving feelings can propel the treatment forward in a creative way, in contrast to *erotised transference*, when patients demand sexual gratification from their helpers. This latter transference manifestation may be part of the patient's desperate attempt to master earlier sexual traumas, and the technical problems involved are likely to involve all the skill the helper can find. At times treatment may break down.

Countertransference

Jung was one of the pioneers of the therapeutic use of countertransference and talked about the 'old idea of the demon of sickness' (Jung, 1921, p. 72). According to this, a sufferer can transmit his or her disease to a healthy person whose powers then subdue the demon. He also used the analogy of a chemical reaction between doctor and patient, which implies not only change in the patient, but a necessary preparedness for change in the helper if the patient is to get well.

It is only since the 1940s that countertransference, that is, the helper's response to the patient's transference, has been the subject of serious scrutiny. Jung (ibid., p. 71) thought it futile for the helper to erect defences of a professional kind against the influence of the patient: 'by doing so, he only denies himself the use of a highly important organ of information'. GPs and counsellors are faced with the task of trying to find a way of handling the emotions that are aroused in them by a patient or colleague, to tolerate misrepresentation and attack, and they may need to sacrifice their own wishes for speedy, definitive returns.

Countertransference applies to those thoughts and feelings experienced by the counsellor that are relevant to the patient's inner world and are a valuable aid to a deeper understanding of the patient. The psychoanalyst Heimann (1950) wrote a seminal paper on the subject, and pointed out that analysts' feelings and associations to their patients' communications are an essential part of understanding the unconscious processes taking place in the patient. Writers today are more cautious and emphasise the danger of overuse of the idea of countertransference, that is, that everything may be put down to the counsellor's feelings about the patient. It is worth remembering Fordham's (1985) helpful distinction between *syntonic countertransference*, where analysts attuned to and empathic with their patients' inner world can find themselves behaving in a way that suggests an extension of the patients' intrapsychic processes, and *illusory countertransference*, which suggests a more neurotic response to patients on the part of analysts.

Working with opposites

Jung's conception of the psyche was of a system that is dynamic, in constant movement and at the same time self-regulating. He called the energy of the psyche *the libido* (with a much broader meaning than that conferred by

Freud). This libido, Jung thought, flows between two opposing poles, like the positive and negative poles of an electric circuit or the diastole and the systole of the heart. Jung usually referred to the opposing poles as *the opposites*. The greater the tension between the pairs of opposites, the greater the energy; without opposition there can be no manifest energy. He wrote that 'the opposites are the ineradicable and indispensable preconditions of all psychic life' (Jung, 1954, para. 206).

His ideas on opposition reveal that growth comes only when the tension between opposites can be resolved: 'science comes to a stop at the frontiers of logic but nature does not – she thrives on ground as yet untrodden by theory. *Venerabilis natura* does not halt at the opposites; she uses them to create, out of opposition, a new birth' (Jung, 1946, para. 524). Pairs of opposites are considered to be irreconcilable. In their natural state they coexist in an undifferentiated way, though the living body usually manages to prevent an excess of psychic disproportion or opposition, except in times of stress. Here the individual may feel at the mercy of first one and then the other of a pair of opposites (the ideal or the denigrated counsellor/mother) and this experience of alternation was thought by Jung to mark the awakening of consciousness. If the tension becomes too great, then some reconciliation or regulation must be found (violent rage is usually succeeded by calm). In extreme cases, where there is a complete failure of the libido to find an outlet, psychosis may be the result. In Jung's view, the two opposites are united through the unconscious formation of a third, 'the symbol'. These uniting or reconciling symbols may appear in dreams or imagination and may take the form of a figure, such the abandoned child or the orphan, which possesses potentials beyond those the conscious mind has yet been able to conceive. Jung believed that it is only the discovery of meaning in human existence that makes it possible to withstand the shifting demands of the opposites (Samuels *et al.*, 1986).

CASE EXAMPLE: SUSAN AND HER MOTHER

Mr and Mrs Allison visit the practice with their fourteen year old daughter Susan, who is extremely distressed and aggressive towards her parents. It becomes clear to the counsellor that Susan has become the repository of all her mother's bad feelings, in contrast to her brother Peter, who is intensely loved by his mother. The tension in this family is enormous because of these overdetermined opposing forces of psychotic proportions. Susan is offering her mother the possibility of 'insight/the third/the resolution' through her angry communication to her mother, and the session with the counsellor provides the opportunity for the tension between these opposing forces in the family to be struggled with more consciously.

In practical terms the possibility of reconciliation between apparently irreconcilable forces is forever present. Living from day to day in the light of this insight brings with it a gift of inestimable value: wisdom. However in order to achieve this wisdom we have to become aware of both poles of every conflict and endure, in full consciousness, the tension created between them. Hopefully some radical shift occurs that leads to the possible birth of 'a third', 'the resolution', a new symbolical synthesis.

Systems theory

Systems theory was developed as a general science of organisations by Ludwig von Bertalanffy (1969) in the 1940s, and later writers have applied it to other social systems (Bateson, 1971; Watzlawick *et al.*, 1974; McCaughan and Palmer, 1994). More recently it has become particularly associated with the practice of family therapy and has achieved success in helping families with stuck patterns of relating to change the ways in which they relate to each other (Carter and McGoldrick, 1986).

When families, work groups or professional organisations encounter problems, they sometimes find they are stuck in futile repetitions of familiar, unsuccessful, attempts to solve the problem. The perspective of general systems thinking can help bring clarity to the situation and often the possibility of making some changes. A system is more than the sum of its parts. Systems theory is interested in the arrangement of these parts and a system is defined as a *self-regulating unit*, where there are patterns of interaction and relationships between persons and groups. It is structured on *feedback*, and feedback responses influence and mould the individual's behaviour. Human social systems such as a family or a GP practice are open systems that consist of hierarchies of subsystems of people or groups. They have a definable but permeable boundary and exchange energy with their surrounding environment. A patient going to the doctor is a member of many systems that exert their unseen influence on the GP and on the GP's system, and *vice versa*.

Systemic thinking aims to understand the whole context in which an event is happening by mapping out the structure of a system, including patterns of interaction, clarification of boundaries, power relationships, and ambiguous agendas. It also looks at the *feedback loops* that link and integrate all components of the system. Feedback is the aggregate of other people's emotional and behavioural responses to an individual's behaviour. Over time, feedback becomes a common pattern recognised by members of the system, and establishes the unwritten *rules of the game*, *scripts of the drama* or *steps of the dance*. For example a GP generally prescribes Prozac rather than referring to the counsellor, or a patient thinks it is better to be depressed than angry. Cause and effect are seen in circular rather than linear terms. The emphasis is not on what has caused an event or which person is to blame, but on identifying the factors that continue to sustain an event.

There are two kinds of feedback, positive and negative. *Positive feedback* leads to the escalation of responses and actions, each bit of feedback prompting more of the behaviour it is intended to change. It leads to 'more of the same', so that the attempted solution becomes part of the problem. For example the more often patients are given Prozac, the less likely they are to think about why they might be feeling depressed; or the more you nag, the more I withdraw. Positive feedback loops often lead to splits and destructiveness. *Negative feedback has a* more regulatory function in a system and triggers mechanisms to counteract too great a deviation from the norm. For example a GP who has had several recent complaints from his patients about having to wait too long in the waiting room for their appointments, has to take two weeks off through overwork. He then decides to reduce the number of patients in each surgery by four.

Homeostasis is the principle that a system strives to maintain itself in a steady state of equilibrium, but this is often counterbalanced by the system's capacity for *transformation* and learning. A GP practice can be creatively adaptational and can increase the complexity of its own organisation over long periods of time, while remaining stable. The survival and continuing effectiveness of the organisation depends on its capacity to learn from feedback. This means it has to be able to modify its structures and practices, and the philosophy that supports them, to meet changing conditions. Primary care has surely had to struggle with an enormous amount of externally generated pressure to change since the GP Contract in 1990.

Sometimes families and organisations cannot make the necessary adaptations and the whole system develops problems. It is helpful to conceptualise the difference between a difficulty and a problem: a *difficulty* is an undesirable state of affairs that can either be resolved by common-sense action or has to be accommodated to and lived with because it is a part of life and there is no solution; a *problem* is an impasse that is created, perpetuated and often made worse by mishandling a difficulty.

In any institution there are many processes that may subtly undermine the development of a self-questioning attitude. For example a common tendency to make the situation look better than it is; inattention to the gap between the way things are said to operate in theory and their actual operation in practice; and the power of group processes, where there are often social rewards for those who avoid challenging current practice. A systemic point of view sees problems and symptoms as helpful communications, thrown up under stress to alert the system as a whole that change has to take place. Sometimes GPs and health professionals unwittingly reenact and mirror the problems of the patients and families they are dealing with. If the system cannot yet adequately respond to the plea, the symptom has to escalate to compel new notice to be taken of the predicament that everyone is locked into unknowingly. It is common to try to locate the cause of difficulty in one place or person (scapegoating), be this a 'difficult' child, parent or colleague.

The central idea behind systems theory is that *change in one part of the system affects and reverberates throughout the whole system.* A new perception of the underlying meaning of redundant patterns, which are no longer adaptive, can free the system as a whole to transform itself and reach a new level of homeostasis. Most change is likely to cause shock, anger, loss and anxiety and will affect everyone in some measure, but even small changes can exert a powerful influence overall, if it is possible to locate at least one 'difference that makes a difference'. (We are grateful to Catherine Crowther, who has kindly made many of her thoughts on systems theory available to us.)

APPENDIX B:
PROFESSIONAL TRAINING FOR COUNSELLING IN PRIMARY CARE

GP training

Forty years ago Michael Balint (1964), a psychiatrist and psychoanalyst, and Enid Balint, a psychoanalyst, pioneered research work with GPs to explore the doctor–patient relationship and the potential for psychotherapy in primary care. Balint saw the GP as the most powerful 'drug' available to treat emotional problems, but pointed out that very little, if any, research had been done on how this 'drug' could most effectively be used, when it might be harmful and what its side effects might be. He outlined a model of listening to and understanding the patient in order to make as complete a diagnosis as possible, using this understanding to make interventions to good therapeutic effect. Whilst only a relatively small number of GPs have actually participated in Balint groups, his influence has undoubtedly permeated medical training, in particular British academic departments of primary care as well as in Germany and the USA, and his approach constitutes a significant attempt to develop training for GPs to use their relationship with patients more productively. The Balint Society and the Tavistock Clinic continue to provide opportunities for learning and the sharing of clinical work in this area.

Training for counsellors

Until recently there has been little training available for counsellors who wish to work in a primary health care setting. As will be evident to the reader of this book, both authors believe firmly that the work is context-specific. To work effectively in primary care means the integration of an institutionally based approach with a more individual, treatment-based approach. Counsellors who persevere with a rigid dyadic model of work that invariably keeps information away from the practice team are likely to become isolated and marginalised within the practice. As a GP once commented: 'what is the point of having counsellors in the practice if they don't talk to you?' (Elder, personal communication).

Similarly, counsellors who work in the same way with all their patients, for example sticking blindly to a six-session model, are unlikely to meet the needs of the practice, as some patients will only want one or two sessions, while others will require occasional sessions over a longer period of time.

Courses

- The Counselling in Primary Care Trust was started in 1991 and is committed to the establishment of a nationwide professional counselling service in medical settings. The Trust sponsors a number of part-time MSc and diploma courses in counselling in primary care, and is involved in various other activities, including research into the training needs of counsellors and other aspects of counselling in primary care; funding the long-term development of assessment, audit and evaluation tools for use in counselling in primary health care; sponsoring conferences and workshops in many parts of the UK; and producing numerous publications, occasional papers and a newsletter.
- The Tavistock Clinic is running a pilot course for counsellors in primary care.
- St George's Hospital runs a large annual conference for counsellors in the field.

Joint training for GPs and counsellors: courses

- For a number of years, the Society of Analytical Psychology (a training institute for Jungian analysts) and the Department of Primary Care and Dentistry at Kings College London have cooperated in putting on workshops for GPs and counsellors working together. These workshops are theme-based and allow professionals from two different disciplines to come together, albeit for brief periods of time, to talk about their differences and anxieties and facilitate more cooperative working relationships. Recently this work has been extended to St Petersburg in Russia, through a grant from the Charities Aid Foundation.
- The British Association of Psychotherapists runs short courses for counsellors and GPs to study the primary care environment.

APPENDIX C: ADDRESSES OF ORGANISATIONS INTERESTED IN COUNSELLING IN PRIMARY CARE

The Society of Analytical Psychology
1 Daleham Gardens
London NW3 5BY

Counselling in Medical Settings Division
British Association Counselling
37a Sheep Street
Rugby
Warwickshire CV21 3BX

The Counselling in Primary Care Trust
Suite 3a
Majestic House
High Street
Staines TW18 4DG

Relate
Herbert Gray College
Little Church Street
Rugby CV21 3AP

The Mental Health Foundation
37 Mortimer Street
London W1N 8PX

The Royal College of General Practitioners
Princes Gate
Hyde Park
London SW7 1PU

British Association of Psychotherapists
37 Mapesbury Road
London NW2 4HJ

Refugee Support Centre
47 South Lambeth Road
London SW8

Tavistock Clinic
120 Belsize Lane
London NW3 5BA

Women's Therapy Centre
10 Manor Gardens
London N7 6JS

Tavistock Marital Studies Institute
120 Belsize Lane
London NW3 5BA

Medical Foundation for the Care of Victims of Torture
96 Grafton Road
London NW5

St George's Department of Primary Care
St. George's Hospital
London SW18

National Primary Care Research and Development Centre
5th Floor
Williamson Building
University of Manchester
Oxford Road
Manchester ML3 9PL

NAFSIYAT: The Inter-Cultural Therapy Centre
278 Seven Sisters Road
London N4 2HY

REFERENCES

Alexander, F. (1950) *Psychosomatic Medicine* (New York: Norton).

Anderson, S. and J. Hasler (1979) 'Counselling in general practice', *Journal Royal College of GPs*, vol. 29, 352–6.

Andrews, G. (1993) 'The essential psychotherapies', *British Journal of Psychiatry*, vol. 162, 447–51.

Andrews, G. (1996) 'Talk that works: The rise of cognitive behaviour therapy', *BMJ*, vol. 313, 1501–2.

Anzieu, D. (1989) *The Skin Ego* (New Haven, CT: Yale University Press).

Ashurst, P. and D. Ward (1983) 'An evaluation of counselling in general practice', *Final Report of the Leverhulme Counselling Project* (London: Mental Health Foundation).

BAC (1993) *Guidelines for the Employment of Counsellors in General Practice*.

Balestieri, M., P. Williams, and G. Wilkinson (1988) 'Specialist mental health treatment in general practice: a meta-analysis', *Psychological Medicine*, vol. 18, 711–17.

Balint, E. (1986) 'The history of training and research in Balint groups', *Psychoanalytic Psychotherapy*, vol. 1, no. 2, 1–9.

Balint, E., M. Courtenay, A. Elder, S. Hull, P. Julian (1993) *The Doctor, the Patient and the Group: Balint Re-visited* (London: Routledge).

Balint, M. (1964) *The Doctor, his patient and the illness*, 2nd edn (London: Pitman).

Bateman, A. and J. Holmes (1995) *Introduction to Psychoanalysis: Contemporary Theory and Practice* (London: Routledge).

Bateson, G. (1971) 'A Systems Approach', *International Journal of Psychiatry*, vol. 9.

Bell, D. (1992) 'Hysteria – a contemporary Kleinian perspective', *British Journal of Psychotherapy*, vol. 9, 2.

Berkowitz, R. (1996) 'Assessment: some issues for counsellors in primary health care', *Psychodynamic Counselling*, vol. 2.

Bertalanffy, L. von (1969) *General Systems Theory* (New York: Brazilier).

Bion, W. (1961) *Experiences in Groups* (London: Tavistock).

BMA (1993) *Medical Ethics Today: Its Practice and Philosophy* (London: BMJ Publishing Group).

Bollas, C. (1987) 'The psychoanalyst and the hysteric', in *The Shadow of the Object: Psychoanalysis of the Unthought Known* (London: Free Association Books).

Bond, T. (1995) 'The nature and outcome of counselling', in J. Keithley and G. Marsh (eds), *Counselling in Primary Health Care* (Oxford: Oxford University Press).

Bourne, S. (1976) 'Second opinion: a study of medical referrals in a seminar for general practitioners at the Tavistock Clinic, London', *Journal Royal College of GPs*, vol. 26, 487–95.

Brenman, E. (1985) 'Hysteria', *International Journal of Psycho-Analysis*, vol. 66, 4.

Brook, A. (1967) 'An experiment in general practitioner/psychiatrist collaboration', *Journal Royal College of GPs*, vol. 13, 126–31.

Brook, A. (1974) 'Supporting the caregivers in the community', lecture given at the symposium 'Psychodynamic Skills in the field of Mental Health', Royal College of Psychiatrists.

Brook, A. and J. Temperley (1976) 'The contribution of a psychotherapist to general practice', *Journal Royal College of GPs*, vol. 26, 86—94.

Burke, M. (1995) 'The role of the counsellor in a GP surgery', unpublished thesis presented for the award of Diploma in Adult Counselling, Birkbeck College, University of London.

Calnan, J. (1991) 'Handling complaints', in *Developing Communication and Counselling Skills in Medicine* (London: Routledge).

Campkin, M. (1995) 'The GP as counsellor', in J. Keithley and G. Marsh (eds), *Counselling in Primary Health Care* (Oxford: Oxford University Press).

Carter, B. and M. McGoldrick (1986) *The Family Life Cycle: a framework for Family Therapy* (New York: Gardner Press).

Coleridge, S. T. (1796) 'Letter to Charles Lloyd, Sr, 14 November', in E. L. Griggs (ed.), *Collected Letters of Samuel Taylor Coleridge*, vol. 1 (Oxford: Clarendon Press, 1966), 256.

Coltart, N. (1992) 'Slouching towards Bethlehem', in *Slouching towards Bethlehem and further Psychoanalytic Explorations* (London: Free Association Books).

Coltart, N. (1993) *How to Survive as a Psychotherapist* (London: Sheldon Press).

Corney, R. (1990) 'Counselling in general practice – does it work?', *Journal of the Royal Society of Medicine*, Discussion Paper, vol. 83, 255–7.

Corney, R. and M. Briscoe (1977) 'Investigation into two different types of attachment schemes', *Social Work Today*, vol. 9, no. 15.

Corney, R. and R. Jenkins (1993) *Counselling in General Practice* (London: Routledge).

Counselling in Medical Settings Working Party (1993) *Guidelines for the Employment of Counsellors in General Practice* (Rugby: British Association of Counselling).

Curtis-Jenkins, G. (1996) *An Introduction to Counselling in Primary Health Care* (Staines: Counselling in Primary Care Trust).

Curtis-Jenkins, G. (1996) *Effectiveness in Counselling Services: Recent Developments in Service Delivery.* (Staines: Counselling in Primary Care Trust).

Dammers, J. and J. Wiener (1995) 'The theory and practice of counselling in the primary health care team', in J. Keithley and G. Marsh (eds), *Counselling and Primary Health Care* (Oxford: Oxford University Press).

DHSS (1987) *Promoting Better Health* (London: HMSO).

Diekstra, R. and M. Jensen (1988) 'Psychology's role in the new health care systems', *Psychology*, vol. 25, no. 3, 344—51.

East, P. (1995) *Counselling in Medical Settings* (Milton Keynes: Open University Press).

Edwards, A. (1983) 'Research studies in the problems of assessment', *Journal of Analytical Psychology*, vol. 28, 4.

Elder, A. (1987) 'Moments of change', in A. Elder, and O. Samuel (eds), *While I'm here, Doctor. A Study of the Doctor Patient Relationship* (London: Tavistock Press).

Elder, A. (1996) 'Primary care and psychotherapy', *Psychoanalytic Psychotherapy* supplement, Conference Proceedings: Future Directions of Psychotherapy in the NHS: Adaptation or Extinction, vol. 10.

Fahy, T. and S. Wessley (1993) 'Should purchasers pay for psychotherapy?', *BMJ*, vol. 307, 576–7.

Fonagy, P. (1993) 'Psychoanalytic and empirical approaches to developmental psychotherapy: can they be usefully integrated?', *Journal Royal Society of Medicine*, vol. 86, 577–81.

Fordham, M. (1974) 'Defences of the self', in *Explorations into the Self*. Library of Analytical Psychology, vol. 7 (London: Academic Press)

Fordham, M. (1985) 'Countertransference', in *Explorations into the Self*, Library of Analytical Psychology , vol. 7 (London: Academic Press).

Forman, J. and E. Fairbairn (1968) *Social Casework in General Medical Practice* (London: Pitman Medical).

Foulger, V. A. L. (1993) 'Letter', *Financial Pulse*, June 8th.

Freeman, G. K. and E. J. Button (1984) 'The clinical psychologist in general practice: a six year study of counselling patterns for psycho-social problems', *Journal Royal College of GPs*, vol. 32, 32–7.

Freud, S. (1895) 'Studies on hysteria', in J. Strachey (ed). *The Standard Edition of the Complete Psychological Works by Sigmund Freud, vol. 2* (London: The Hogarth Press and the Institute of Psychoanalysis).

Freud, S. (1923) 'The ego and the id', in J. Strachey (ed). *The Standard Edition of the Complete Psychological Works by Sigmund Freud, vol. 19* (London: The Hogarth Press and the Institute of Psychoanalysis).

Garelick, A. (1994) 'Psychotherapy assessment: theory and practice', *Psychoanalytic Psychotherapy*, vol. 8, no. 2.

Garelick, A. and J. Wiener (1996) 'Paranoia or adaptation? The implications of a King's Fund review on a psychotherapy department', *Psychoanalytic Psychotherapy*, vol. 10, no. 3.

GMC (1993) *Professional Conduct and Discipline: Fitness to Practice*, paragraphs 42–3 (London: GMC).

Goldberg, E. and J. Neill (1972) *Social Work in General Practice* (London: George Allan and Unwin).

Göpfert, M. and B. Barnes (1994) 'Counsellors and secondary mental health care', unpublished presentation, Liverpool Psychotherapy and Consultation Service.

Graham, H. and M. Sher (1976) 'Social work in general practice', *Journal Royal College of GPs* , vol. 26, 95–105.

Graham, H. and M. Sher (1976) 'Social work in general practice', *British Journal of Social Work*, vol. 6, no. 2.

Guggenbühl-Craig, A (1982) *Power in the Helping Professions* (Dallas, Texas: Spring Publications).

Halmos, P. (1965) *Faith in the Counsellors* (London: Constable).

Harris C., and M. Pringle (1994) 'Do general practitioner computer systems assist in medical audit?', *Family Practice*, vol. 11, 51–6.

Heimann, P. (1950) 'On countertransference', *Psycho-Analysis*, vol. 31.

Hinshelwood, R. (1987) 'The psychotherapist's role in large psychiatric institutions', *Psychoanalytic Psychotherapy*, vol. 2, no. 3, 212.

Hinshelwood, R. (1995) 'Psychodynamic formulation in assessment for psychoanalytic psychotherapy', in C. Mace (ed.), *The Art and Science of Assessment in Psychotherapy* (London: Routledge).

Hinshelwood, R. (1996) 'The relationship between psychiatry and psychotherapy', *Psychoanalytic Psychotherapy*, supplement, Conference Proceedings: Future Directions of Psychotherapy in the NHS: Adaptation or Extinction, vol. 10.

Hobson, R. (1985) *Forms of Feeling: The Heart of Psychotherapy* (London: Tavistock).

Holmes, J. (1995) 'How I assess for psychoanalytic psychotherapy', in C. Hale (ed.), *The Art and Science of Assessment in Psychotherapy* (London: Routledge).

Hornby, S. (1993) *Collaborative Care* (Oxford: Blackwell).

House R. (1993) 'Counselling in general practice: a view from humanistic psychology', unpublished paper.

Hughes, S. (1993) 'Is GP counselling a worthwhile service?', *Financial Pulse*, 8 May

Ives, G. (1979) 'Psychological treatment in general practice', *Journal Royal College of GPs*, , vol. 29, 343–51

Jewell, T. (1993) 'Counselling in general practice', *BMJ*, vol. 306.

Jung, C. G. (1916) 'The transcendent function', in C. G. Jung, *The Collected Works, vol. 8*. Ed. by H. Read, M. Fordham, G. Adler (London: Routledge & Kegan Paul).

Jung, C. G. (1921) 'Problems of modern psychotherapy'. in C. G. Jung *The Collected Works, vol. 16*. Ed. by H. Read, M. Fordham, G. Adler (London: Routledge & Kegan Paul).

Jung, C. G. (1934) 'Definitions', in C. G. Jung, *The Collected Works, vol. 6*, 747. Ed. by H. Read, M. Fordham, G. Adler (London: Routledge & Kegan Paul).

Jung, C. G. (1946) 'The psychology of the transference', in C. G. Jung, *The Collected Works, vol. 16*. Ed. by H. Read, M. Fordham, G. Adler (London: Routledge & Kegan Paul).

Jung, C. G. (1954) 'The personification of the opposites', in C. G. Jung, *The Collected Works, vol. 14*, 206. Ed. by H. Read, M. Fordham, G. Adler (London: Routledge & Kegan Paul).

Keithley, J. and G. Marsh (eds) (1995) *Counselling in Primary Health Care* (Oxford: Oxford University Press).

Kernberg, O. (1984) *Severe Personality Disorders: Therapeutic Strategies* (Newhaven, CT: Yale University Press).

Khan, M. M. R. (1983) 'Grudge and the hysteric', in *Hidden Selves: Between Theory and Practice in Psychoanalysis* (London: Hogarth Press).

Klein, M. (1935) 'Contribution to the psychogenesis of manic depressive states', in *The writings of Melanie Klein, vol. 1, Love, Guilt and Reparation* (London: Hogarth) pp. 262–89

Klein, M. (1946) 'Notes on some schizoid mechanisms', in P. Heimann, S. Isaacs and J. Riviere (eds), *Developments in Psychoanalysis* (London: Hogarth).

Klein, M. (1952) 'Some theoretical conclusions regarding the emotional life of the infant', in Klein *et al.* (eds), *Developments in Psychoanalysis* (London: Hogarth).

Klein, M. (1975) 'Our Adult World and its Roots in Infancy', in *Envy and Gratitude and other works 1946–1963* (London: Hogarth Press and the Institute of Pschoanalysis).

Koch, H. (1979) 'Evaluation of behaviour therapy interventions in general practice', *Journal Royal College of GPs*, vol. 29, 343–51.

Kohut, H. (1984) a chapter in A. Goldberg and P. Stepansky (eds), *How does Analysis Cure?* (Chicago, Ill.: University of Chicago Press).

Lambert, K. (1981) *Analysis, Repair and Individuation*, Library of Analytical Psychology, vol. 5 (London: Academic Press).

Laplanche, J. and J. B. Pontalis (1980) *The Language of Psycho-analysis* (London: Hogarth Press and the Institute of Psycho-Analysis).

Lawrence, G. (1994) *The Politics of Salvation and the Politcs of Revelation: What makes Consultancy Work?* (London: South Bank University Press).

Limentani, A. (1989) 'The assessment of analysability: a major hazard for selection in psychoanalysis', in *Between Freud and Klein: The psychoanalytic quest for truth* (London: Free Association Books).

Lincoln, Y. and E. Guba (1985) *Naturalistic Inquiry* (Newbury Park, CA: Sage).

Locke, D. C. (1989) 'Increasing multicultural awareness: a comprehensive model', in *Multicultural Aspects of Counselling series* (Newbury Park, CA: Sage)

Main, T. (1989a) 'The ailment', in J. Johns (ed), *The Ailment and other Psychoanalytic Essays* (London: Free Association Books).

Main, T. (1989b) 'Some medical defences against involvement with patients', in J. Johns (ed.), *The Ailment and other Psychoanalytic Essays* (London: Free Association Books).

Malan, D. (1979) *Individual Psychotherapy and the Science of Psychodynamics* (New York: Phenom).

Martin, E. and P. Martin (1985) 'Changes in psychological diagnosis and prescription in a practice employing a counsellor', *Family Practice*, vol. 4, 241–3.

Martin, E. and H. Mitchell (1983) 'A counsellor in general practice: a one year survey', *Journal Royal College of GPs*, vol. 33, 366–7.

McCaughan, N. and B. Palmer (1994) *Systems Thinking for Harassed Managers* (London: Karnac).

McDougall, J. (1989) *Theatres of the Body: A Psychoanalytic approach to Psychosomatic Illness* (London: Free Association Books).

McLeod, J. (1988) 'The work of counsellors in general practice', Occasional Paper no. 37 (London: Royal College of General Practitioners).

Meltzer, D. (1968) 'Terror, persecution, dread: a dissection of paranoid anxieties', *International Journal of Psycho-Analysis*, vol. 49.

Menzies Lyth, I. (1988) *Containing Anxiety in Institutions: Selected Essays* (London: Free Association Books).

Miller, E., J. Broadbent, A. Day, D. Khaleelee, D. Pym (1983) Psychotherapists and the process of profession building. Report based on 'Psychotherapists and Society: A workshop to share experience of the professional role'. For OPUS: an organiation for promoting understanding in society.

Morgan, D. (1988) *Focus Groups as Qualitative Research* (Newbury Park, CA: Sage).

Morrison, B. (1993) *And when did you last see your father?* (London: Granta).

Obholzer, A. (1988) 'Management and psychic reality', in F. Gabelnick and A. W. Carr (eds), *Contributions to Social and Political Science: Proceedings of the First International Symposium on Group Relations* (Keble College), (Washington: A. K. Rice Institute), 15–18.

Obholzer, A. (1994) 'Fragmentation and integration in a school for physically handicapped children', in *The Unconscious at Work: Individual and Organisational Stress in the Human Services* (Routledge).

Ogden, T. (1989) 'The initial analytic meeting', in *The Primitive Edge of Experience* (Northvale, NJ and London: Jason Aronson).

Pereira Gray, D. (1996) 'The role of counsellors in general practice', Occasional Paper no. 74, Editor's Preface (Royal College of General Practitioners, November).

Pietroni, M. (1995) 'Inner-city general practice: the experience of one day's counselling', *Psychodynamic Counselling*, vol. 1, no. 3, 449.

Pringle, M. (1993) 'A counsellor in every practice?', *BMJ*, vol. 36, 22.

Ratoff, L. and B. Pearson (1970) 'Social casework in general practice: an alternative approach', *BMJ*, vol. 2, 475–7.

Rosenfeld, H. (1964) 'On the psychopathology of narcissism: a clinical approach', *International Journal of Psycho-Analysis*, vol. 45.

Rowland, N. and A. Tolley (1995) 'Economic evaluation', in J. Keithley and G. Marsh (eds), *Counselling in Primary Health Care* (Oxford: Oxford University Press).

Samuels, A., B. Shorter and F. Plaut (1986) *A Critical Dictionary of Jungian Analysis* (London and New York: Routledge & Kegan Paul).

Samuels, A. (1989) 'Introduction', in *Psychopathology: Contemporary Jungian Perspectives* (London: Karnac).

Schachter, J. (1990) unpublished paper 'Referrals, assesments and management in the practice', given at a workshop: Emotional problems in General Practice: who needs counselling?, January 1990 (The Human Perspective and Kings College School of Medicine and Dentistry) October Gallery, London.

Sher, M. (1977) 'Short term contracts in general medical practice', in J. Hutten (ed), *Short-Term Contracts in Social Work* (London: Routledge & Kegan Paul).

Sibbald, B., J. Addington Hall, D. Brenneman and P. Freeling (1993) 'Counsellors in English and Welsh general practices: their nature and distribution', *BMJ*, vol. 306, 29–33.

Sibbald, B., J. Addington Hall, D. Brenneman and P. Freeling (1996) 'The role of counsellors in general practice', Occasional Paper no. 74 (London: Royal College of General Practitioners, November).

Steiner, J. (1982) 'Perverse relationships between parts of the self: a clinical illustration', *International Journal of Psycho-Analysis*, vol. 63.

Steiner, J. (1993) 'Problems of psychoanalytic technique: patient centered and analyst centered interpretations', in *Psychic Retreats* (London: Routledge).

Stern, D. N. (1985) *The Interpersonal World of the Infant* (New York: Basic Books).

Temperley, J. (1978) 'Psychotherapy in the setting of general medical practice', *British Journal of Medical Psychology*, vol. 51, 139–45.

Thomas, K., J. Carr, L. Westlake, B. Williams *et al.* (1991) 'Use of non-orthodox and conventional healthcare in Great Britain', *BMJ* , vol. 302, 207–210.

Watzlawick, P., J. Weakland and R. Fisca (1974) *Change: principles of problem formation and problem resolution* (New York: W.W. Norton).

Waydenfeld, D. and S. W. Waydenfeld (1980) 'Counselling in general practice', *Journal Royal College of GPs*, vol. 30, 671–77.

Wiener, J. (1994) 'Looking out and looking in: some reflections on "body talk" in the consulting room', *Journal of Analytical Psychology*, vol. 39, 3.

Wiener, J. (1996) 'Primary care and psychotherapy', *Psychoanalytic Psychotherapy*, supplement, Conference Proceedings: Future Directions of Psychotherapy in the NHS: Adaptation or Extinction, vol. 10.

Williams, M. (1963) 'The indivisibility of the personal and the collective unconscious', *Journal of Analytical Psychology*, vol. 8, no. 1.

Winnicott, D. W. (1965) *The Maturational Process and the Facilitating Environment* (London: Hogarth).

Winnicott, D. W. (1996) *Playing and Reality* (London and New York: Routledge).

Zinkin, L. (1991) 'The Klein connection in the London school: the search for origins', *Journal of Analytical Psychology*, vol. 36, 1.

INDEX

'stranger anxiety': and new
counsellors 25
stress
and cost-effectiveness 152–3
in GPs 1–2, 5, 6, 54–6
and organisational dysfunction 152
in patients 3, 5, 14, 18, 28, 45, 59
stress clinics 2
supportive counselling 87–8, 108–9
surgeries *see* practices, GP
systems theory/systemic
approaches xxi, 97–8, 152, 166–7

Tavistock Clinic 4, 168, 169
teamwork and primary care 5, 6, 8
criticisms of 21–2
interprofessional 127–8
and meetings 27
models of 18–21
see also GPs: collaboration/
communication with counsellors
teenagers 7, 63
Temperley, J. 4
terminal illnesses 14, 77
terminations, pregnancy 77, 86
therapeutic styles/therapies 91
flexible 3, 8–9, 92
mixing 39, 45–6, 61, 106
see also psychoanalysis;
psychodynamic approaches;
training in counselling; treatment
Thomas, K., Carr, J., Westlake, L.,
Williams, B. *et al.* 128
thyroid gland disease 113
time restrictions 9, 32, 49–50, 60, 140
Tolley, A. *see* Rowland, N.
training in counselling:
and counsellors' backgrounds 2–3,
17, 38, 53, 75, 106, 139–40
and counsellors' identity 38
for GPs 56–7, 168, 169
specific xii, 43, 38–9, 44–5, 46–7, 48,
128–9, 168–9

'transcendent function' 74
transference 74, 80, 90, 112, 163–4
erotic 118, 164
psychotic 163
'split' 140
traumatised patients 78
treatment
and assessment 80–4
brief therapy 86, 107–8
and collaboration with GPs 85–6
factors relevant to 85
long-term 87
occasional (supportive)
sessions 87–8, 108–9
shared care (counsellor and
GP) 88–9
and therapeutic styles 3, 8–9, 39,
45–6, 61, 106
and time restrictions 42, 49–50, 140

ulcerative colitis 113
unconscious processes 41, 158
and responses to patients 54, 64–6
United Kingdom Council for
Psychotherapy (UKCP) xxiv, 72
United Kingdom Register for
Counsellors (UKRC) xxiv

vitality affects 114–15

Ward, D. *see* Ashurst, P.
Watzlawick, P. 166
Waydenfeld, D. and S.W. 18, 151
Wessley, S. *see* Fahy, T.
Westlake, L. *see* Thomas, K.
Wiener, J. xii, xix, xx–xxiv, 11, 114
see also Dammers, J.; Garelick, A.
Williams, B. *see* Thomas, K.
Williams, M. 158
Winnicott, D.W. xxi, 109, 157, 159

Zinkin, L. 114